I0113290

A MEDIEVAL BOOK
OF MAGICAL STONES
The Peterborough Lapidary

Edited and Translated
by

Francis Young

𝕿EXTS IN 𝕮ARLY
𝕸ODERN 𝕸AGIC

Introduction, translation and notes © Francis Young 2016

All rights reserved. No part of this publication may be reproduced, stored in a retrieval system or transmitted in any form or by any means, electronic, mechanical, photocopying, recording or otherwise without the prior permission of the publisher.

Francis Young has asserted his moral right under the Copyright, Designs and Patents Act, 1988, to be identified as the author of this translation and the accompanying introduction and notes.

First published 2016
Texts in Early Modern Magic
Cambridge, United Kingdom

A catalogue record for this book is available from the British Library

ISBN 978-0-9926404-4-6

For Sarah

Fig. 1. Peterborough Cathedral. Photograph by the editor.

PREFACE

The Peterborough Lapidary (Cambridge University Library MS Peterborough Cathedral 33, fols 1r–16v) is a late fifteenth-century treatise, mostly in Middle English, on the 'virtues' (magical properties) of stones and gems. It is the longest and most comprehensive of all medieval English lapidaries. In spite of the Peterborough Lapidary's importance, no translation of the text into modern English has been available until now. Hitherto, the only edition of the original Middle English and Latin text was that edited in 1933 by Joan Evans and Mary S. Serjeantson as volume 190 in the Original Series of the Early English Texts Society. Evans' and Serjeantson's interest in the text was philological and their edition was intended for study by scholars of Middle English; consequently they provided no translation. The result is that this and other lapidaries are relatively inaccessible to – and sometimes overlooked by – scholars outside the field of English literature, such as historians of science, medicine and magic.

This two-column edition provides the first translation of the Peterborough Lapidary into modern English alongside the original Middle English text, as well as attempting to remedy some of the faults of the earlier edition by correcting a small number of errors. A detailed introduction, drawing on the latest scholarship, introduces the lapidary tradition and sets the Peterborough Lapidary within the wider context of medieval science, medicine and magic. For this new edition I have carefully compared Evans' and Serjeantson's 1933 edition with the original manuscript in Cambridge University Library to produce a new and, I trust, accurate text. I am grateful to the staff of the Manuscripts Room of Cambridge University Library and I acknowledge with thanks the kind permission of the Dean and Chapter of Peterborough Cathedral to produce a new edition of the Peterborough Lapidary. I am especially grateful to the Rev. Canon Tim Alban-Jones and the acting Dean, the Rev. Canon Jonathan Baker. I thank the Portable Antiquities Scheme, the British Museum and Wellcome Images for permitting the reproduction of the figures.

Naturally, I take full responsibility for any and all remaining errors in the Middle English and Latin text, as well as for any errors or ill-judged choices in the translation.

Serpentine Green, Peterborough
October 2016

vii

CONTENTS

LIST OF FIGURES AND TABLES

Cover Image: An Anglo-Saxon pendant (opal set in gold c. 650–700CE) found at Binbrook, Lincolnshire © The Portable Antiquities Scheme

Fig. 1: Peterborough Cathedral

Fig. 2: White Kennett (1660–1728), Dean (1707–18) and then Bishop (1718–28) of Peterborough

Fig. 3: West Porch of Peterborough Cathedral

Fig. 4: An Anglo-Saxon crystal ball pendant © The British Museum

Fig. 5: Apothecary's jar for storing fragments of emerald, c. 1700 © Wellcome Images

Fig. 6: Apothecary's jar for storing fragments of sapphire, 1600–1625 © Wellcome Images

Fig. 7: Crystal pendant owned by John Dee (1527–1608/9) © Wellcome Images

Fig. 8: The lapidary at work, engraving by B. L. Prevost after J. N. F. Boucher (eighteenth century) © Wellcome Images

INTRODUCTION

The Peterborough Lapidary is the longest of all medieval English treatises on the 'virtues' (occult properties) of stones. It is named after the library of Peterborough Cathedral, which has owned the manuscript since at least the early eighteenth century (although it has been on permanent loan to Cambridge University Library since 1970). The manuscript consists of descriptions of the properties of 128 stones and gems in 145 entries (seventeen of the stones have two or more entries each) and was compiled in the late fifteenth century. Knowledge of the occult properties of stones and gems was essential to the practice of medicine as well as natural and ritual magic, and the authors of lapidaries shared with practitioners of natural magic a concern for 'proving' the virtues of natural things by experiment, rather than relying purely on the testimony of antiquity. Lapidaries thus occupy an important place in the history of science, medicine and magic.

The lapidary tradition

The first lapidary was a short treatise *De lapidibus* ('Of Stones') by the Greek philosopher Theophrastus of Eresos (c. 371–c. 287 BCE), who succeeded Aristotle as head of the Lycaeum in Athens. Theophrastus, as the inheritor of Aristotelian natural philosophy, extended the Aristotelian project of categorising and understanding animals into the realms of plants and minerals. Theophrastus' writings on stones made their way into the work of other authors, such as Pliny the Elder, and from there into the great early medieval encyclopaedias (attempts at universal collections of knowledge) such as the *Etymologies* of Isidore of Seville (560–636).

The first dedicated medieval prose treatise on stones was Albert the Great's *De mineralibus* ('Of Minerals'), which appeared in around 1260. However, Albert's work was preceded by the poem *De lapidibus* ('Of Stones') by Marbod, Bishop of Rennes (1035–1133).[1] Marbod's *De lapidibus* was 'the *Urtext* for the larger portion of verse and prose lapidaries in western Europe', and was 'one of the first to draw the secular audience into the lapidary tradition'.[2] According to Steven Walton,

> Medieval lapidaries usually dealt with one to three dozen stones, describing their appearance and listing their magical properties together with their medical properties – often confounding the two. They rarely deal with the origins of the stones, and never with their formation or composition. Such compilations served a twofold purpose throughout the Middle Ages. First, they maintained the guise of preserving and commenting on antique knowledge so cherished by the Schoolmen and, second, they fitted well into the larger medieval phenomenon of *Rezeptliterature* through which most information on natural remedies, processes, and substances passed.[3]

It is worth noting that the Peterborough Lapidary hardly fits Walton's description of a typical medieval lapidary; it is four times longer than average and frequently shows an interest in the origins – and even formation – of the stones it describes.

Latin lapidaries appeared in England from the twelfth century onwards, but unlike many other forms of learned literature, lapidaries were translated into the vernacular early on. Indeed, the earliest surviving vernacular lapidary in Europe (British Library MS Cotton Tiberius A. iii) is in Old English.[4] However, vernacular lapidaries were also produced in England in the *lingua franca* of the clergy and nobility, Norman French, from the thirteenth century onwards. This might be expected of expensive manuscripts destined for the aristocracy, gentry and clergy.[5] In the fourteenth and fifteenth centuries lapidaries, like 'recipe' collections, became 'an increasingly common, even an essential part of the furnishings of middle class and noble

---

[1] For a good overview of the history of the lapidary tradition see Walton, S. A., 'Theophrastus on *Lyngurium*: Medieval and Early Modern Lore from the Classical Lapidary Tradition', *Annals of Science* 58 (2001), pp. 357–79, at pp. 359–62.

[2] Ibid., p. 361.

[3] Ibid., p. 362.

[4] Fulk, R. D. and Cain, C. M. (eds), *A History of Old English Literature* (Oxford: Blackwell, 2003), pp. 157–9.

[5] On Anglo-Norman lapidaries see Vising, J., *Anglo-Norman Language and Literature* (Oxford: Oxford University Press, 1923); Dean, R. J., *Anglo-Norman Literature: A Guide to Texts and Manuscripts* (London: Anglo-Norman Texts Society, 1999).

households'.[6] The wide appeal of lapidaries probably derived from an inevitable human fascination with precious things, but it may also be ascribed to the fact that owning a stone with occult properties offered the chance of easily portable magic without the need for extensive ritual and preparation. In addition to their secular popularity, lapidaries also appeared in the libraries of medieval monasteries,[7] and it is possible that the Peterborough Lapidary was owned by the medieval Abbey of Peterborough before it was in the library of Peterborough Cathedral.

Lapidaries occupy an ambiguous position in medieval literature, somewhere between forbidden books of magic on the one hand and orthodox books of natural medicine on the other. John Riddle identified three kinds of lapidaries: 'scientific' or medical lapidaries, magical-astrological lapidaries, and Christian lapidaries focussing on exegesis of Biblical passages pertaining to precious stones.[8] The lapidaries stand at the head of the modern sciences of geology, mineralogy and gemmology, because their compilers were interested in the physical properties of stones and how they came to be. Lapidaries also occupy a place in the history of pharmacology and medicine, since 'lithotherapy' (the attempt to use stones for healing) involved grinding up stones to create drugs to be physically ingested.

However, lapidaries were also texts of magic or 'lithomancy', offering readers the chance to take advantage of the occult properties of stones, which were believed to operate at a distance. Lapidaries identified stones that could be used for divination and advocated the wearing of stones as amulets around the neck or set into finger rings, promising marvellous results. As such, it is in the lapidaries that we find the origins of the enduring British fascination with stones as sources of spiritual power, which – judging from the number of 'New Age' shops selling healing and empowering crystals – is still as strong as ever.

There was also a financial dimension to lapidaries. It is no accident that the same word used for a treatise on the properties of

---

[6] Keiser, G. R., 'The Sources of the Peterborough Lapidary' in C. De Backer (ed.), *Cultuurhistorische Caleidoscoop: aangeboden aan Prof. Dr. Willy L. Braekman* (Ghent: Stichting Mens en Kultuur, 1992), pp. 342–8, at p. 348.

[7] Page, S., *Magic in the Cloister: Pious Motives, Illicit Interests, and Occult Approaches to the Medieval Universe* (University Park, PA: Pennsylvania State University Press, 2013), pp. 10–11.

[8] Riddle, J. M., 'Lithotherapy in the Middle Ages: Lapidaries considered as Medical Texts', *Pharmacy in History* 12:2 (1970), pp. 39–50, at pp. 39–40.

stones – lapidary – was also used to describe an individual who cut, polished and sold stones. The lapidaries, highlighting as they did the rarity and value of certain stones and insisting that many of them had to be set in gold, intentionally or unintentionally promoted the jewellery trade. In the Middle Ages and early modern period, even jewels set in crowns and sceptres were often put there as much for the occult virtues of the stone as for purely aesthetic reasons.

We may no longer be inclined to ascribe occult properties to precious stones, but the intangible, almost supernatural glamour associated with valuable and expensive stones, such as diamonds, is an enduring feature of contemporary culture that we can readily recognise in medieval lapidaries. Thanks to the lapidaries, the idea of precious stones with magical powers occurs again and again in English literature, from the fourteenth-century *Pearl* poem to J. R. R. Tolkien's Arkenstone and the Resurrection Stone of *Harry Potter and the Deathly Hallows*. The lapidaries transmitted Greek and Roman knowledge about stones in an easily accessible vernacular, and although ancient wisdom was often recycled by the lapidaries in a debased form,[9] this did not mean that they were any less highly regarded by seekers after hidden knowledge in the sixteenth and seventeenth centuries. The Peterborough Lapidary cannot be categorised simply as a medical, magical or Christian lapidary; like most fifteenth-century lapidaries, it contains elements of all three traditions, but the length of the Peterborough Lapidary makes it exceptional.

Scholarship on the Peterborough Lapidary

The Peterborough Lapidary seems to have been an unknown text before its discovery by Evans and Serjeantson in the 1930s. Evans and Serjeantson, who first named the text 'The Peterborough Lapidary', identified the text as late fifteenth-century, on the basis of linguistic and palaeographical features.[10] In their critical notes on the text, they identified thirteen sources used by the compiler:[11]

1. The *Etymologies* of Isidore of Seville ('Ised' in the text)
2. The *Liber lapidum* ('Book of Stones') of Marbod of Rennes

---

[9] See Walton (2001), pp. 357–79.

[10] Evans, J. and Serjeantson, M. S. (eds), *Mediaeval English Lapidaries*, Early English Texts Society 190 (Oxford: Early English Texts Society, 1933), pp. 10–11.

[11] Ibid., p. 160.

3. John Trevisa's translation of the *De proprietatibus rerum* ('Of the Properties of Things') of Bartholomaeus Anglicus ('Bartholomewe' in the text)
4. The Latin text of *De proprietatibus rerum*
5. The *Liber mineralium* ('Book of Minerals') of Albert the Great ('Albertus' in the text)
6. *De lapidibus preciosis* ('Of Precious Stones') of Thomas of Cantimpré
7. Jean Mandeville's *Lapidaire en francoys* ('Lapidary in French')
8. The Lapidary of King Phillip
9. The London Lapidary of King Phillip
10. The First Anglo-Norman Verse Lapidary
11. The Alphabetical Lapidary
12. The First Anglo-Norman Prose Lapidary
13. The Second Anglo-Norman Prose Lapidary

Evans and Serjeantson were primarily interested in identifying parallel passages between the Peterborough Lapidary and one or more of these sources.[12] However, this method did not prove entirely effective owing to the still-limited state of knowledge of lapidaries at the time, and the editors were forced to concede that they were unable to identify descriptions of six stones (20, 48, 54, 55, 92 and 119) in any of the known sources, along with many individual properties of known stones that they were unable to trace to other lapidaries. However, Evans and Serjeantson were successful in demonstrating that the compiler of the Peterborough Lapidary did *not* have direct access to many of the authors he cites – such as Pliny the Elder and Platearius – except via secondary sources.

In 1943 Leo Henkin dismissed the Peterborough Lapidary as 'without doubt merely an English transcription of the Alphabetical Lapidary',[13] missing the fact that the manuscript, although broadly alphabetical in arrangement, does not correspond exactly to any other lapidary. As the most extensive of the vernacular lapidaries, the Peterborough Lapidary has mainly attracted attention from scholars of English literature. As early as 1959, Francis Manley observed in an

---

[12] Ibid. pp. 160–79.
[13] Henkin, L. J., 'The Carbuncle in the Adder's Head', *Modern Language Notes* 58:1 (1943), pp. 34–9, at p. 38.

article on Chaucer that coral's ability to attract love is first mentioned in the Peterborough Lapidary.[14]

The Peterborough Lapidary is the only vernacular lapidary to privilege pearls as important stones; generally speaking, pearls 'do not rank high' in medieval lapidaries, partly because the pearl does not appear among the stones that form the foundation of the heavenly city in the Book of Revelation.[15] However, the compiler of the Peterborough Lapidary thought a great deal of them, granting emerald only 'the third dignity after pearls' (p. 68), and describing pearl as 'the chief of all stones that are white and precious' (p. 75). Although the fourteenth-century alliterative Middle English poem *The Pearl* pre-dates the transcription of the Peterborough Lapidary by about a century, scholars have made use of the lapidary to argue for the significance of pearls in medieval English culture.[16] Similarly, Joel Fredell identifies the philosophers' stone (described by the fifteenth-century monk-poet John Lydgate in *Secrees of Old Philisofferes* as 'of Colour ... Sumtyme Cytrynade') with the 'lesser' jacinth of the Peterborough Lapidary.[17]

A rare instance of a detailed study of the content of the Peterborough Lapidary for its own sake, rather than as a resource for understanding medieval literature, is Christopher Duffin's meticulous examination of all medieval references to the 'cock's stone', known as alectorius, which is treated early on in the lapidary. Although at one point Duffin mistakenly dated the Peterborough Lapidary to the late sixteenth century,[18] he noticed distinctive features of the lapidary's description of the stone. The Peterborough compiler describes the colour of alectorius as 'shynynge lik to crystal water' (p. 8), in contrast to other commentators who compared the stone either to water or

---

[14] Manley, F., 'Chaucer's Rosary and Donne's Bracelet: Ambiguous Coral', *Modern Language Notes* 74:5 (1959), pp. 385–88, at p. 387.

[15] Davenport, T., 'Jewels and Jewellers in "Pearl"', *The Review of English Studies*, New Series 59:241 (2008), pp. 508–20, at p. 519.

[16] On the literary significance of the Peterborough Lapidary see also Taylor, P. B., 'Chaucer's Eye of the Lynx and the Limits of Vision', *The Chaucer Review* 28:1 (1993), pp. 67–77, at p. 77n.; Bloomfield, J., 'Aristotelian Luminescence, Thomistic Charity: Vision, Reflection and Self-love in "Pearl"', *Studies in Philology* 108:2 (2011), pp. 165–88, at p. 167n. In the 1970s Penelope Doob drew on the Peterborough Lapidary to decode an obscure allusion in Chaucer's *Troilus and Criseyde* (Doob, P., 'Chaucer's "Corones Tweyne" and the Lapidaries', *The Chaucer Review* 7:2 (1972), pp. 85–96, at p. 89).

[17] Fredell, J. 'Alchemical Lydgate', *Studies in Philology* 107:4 (2010), pp. 429–64, at p. 435. The compiler of the Peterborough Lapidary shows no interest in alchemy, however.

[18] Duffin, C. J., 'The Cock's Stone', *Folklore* 118:3 (2007), pp. 325–41, at p. 334.

crystal.[19] The Peterborough Lapidary, unlike other lapidaries which suggested that the stone would appear in the 'capon's womb' three, four, six or ten years after its castration, offered seven years.[20] In common with other lapidaries, the Peterborough Lapidary ascribes to alectorius the power of granting its bearer victory in battle, but distinctively it recommends that the stone should be placed over the 'helme' in battle.[21] In claiming that alectorius excites lechery the Peterborough compiler directly contradicts the North Midland Lapidary, which says the stone suppresses it.[22] The Peterborough Lapidary also considers alectorius favourable for conception and lactation.[23]

In a separate article, Duffin traced the folklore of fish otoliths (mineral accretions found in fish) and identified the Peterborough Lapidary as the only text that suggests holding the otolith cinaedia in the mouth in order to prevent storms.[24] Although Duffin's scholarship is focussed narrowly on just two stones mentioned in the Peterborough Lapidary, it is significant insofar as it appears to show that the compiler did not just rely slavishly on his sources, but also improvised (or at least drew from sources now lost) his own interpretations. The problem of the unknown sources of the Peterborough Lapidary was tackled by George Keiser in the 1980s and '90s, first in the introduction to his edition of a hitherto unknown Middle English version of the lapidary known as Þe Boke of Stones, and then later in a chapter devoted to the Peterborough Lapidary.[25]

Keiser concluded that the new lapidary he had discovered, Newberry MS 32.9, was a southern English translation of the French Li livre des pierres, called (mistakenly) by Evans and Serjeantson 'The London Lapidary of King Phillip'. Keiser demonstrated that this southern version of Þe Boke of Stones, shared a common source with the Peterborough Lapidary. He offered three instances when the Peterborough Lapidary closely paralleled the Newberry text: the claim that chrysolite threaded on a donkey's bristle will allow someone 'to go among devils' (p. 19); the claim that bloodstone preserves the

---

[19] Ibid., p. 327.
[20] Ibid., p. 331.
[21] Ibid., p. 332.
[22] Ibid., p. 333.
[23] Ibid. p. 335.
[24] Duffin, C. J., 'Fish Otoliths and Folklore: A Survey', *Folklore* 118:1 (2007), pp. 78–90, at pp. 81, 86.
[25] Keiser, G. R. (ed.), *The Middle English 'Boke of Stones': The Southern Version* (Brussels: Omirel, UFSAL, 1984); Keiser (1992), pp. 342–8.

reputation, staunches blood and is an antidote to venom (p. 40); and the claim that pure green jasper is more valuable than stones with black spots (p. 53).[26] Keiser argued that the compiler of the Peterborough Lapidary conflated 'portions of Þe Boke of Stones and portions of Book XVI of Trevisa's translation of De proprietatibus rerum [by Bartholomaeus Anglicus] (along with portions of still other works)'. Both the Peterborough Lapidary and the Newberry text of Þe Boke of Stones 'represent that informative fusion, ideal by medieval standards, of the learning of the ancients and Christian enlightenment, by which it was possible to discover in the wonders of the created world a mirror of the wonders of its Creator'.[27] Keiser provided an appendix in which he identified fifty passages in the Peterborough Lapidary that drew on the southern Boke of Stones.

In his 1992 article on the sources of the Peterborough Lapidary, Keiser identified a number of passages in which the compiler was indebted to John Trevisa's translation of Anglicus' De proprietatibus rerum, for instance in his description of 'Absittus' (apsyctos) as 'streaked with red streaks and red veins'.[28] Keiser was the first to notice that the Peterborough compiler's account of 'Andromia' is likewise dependent on Trevisa, and Keiser concluded that the Peterborough scribe 'slavishly' followed the source he was copying.[29] However, the Peterborough lapidarist had a strong tendency to conflate material drawn from Trevisa's translation of Anglicus with material from the lost version of the southern Boke of Stones on which he relied, resulting in his confusion of the properties of 'nitrum' with 'vitrum' (glass) in the lengthy description of 'uytrum' (glass).[30] Keiser also spotted similarities between the Peterborough compiler's readings of Trevisa and those found in another manuscript in Cambridge University Library, MS Ii.5.41. Indeed, the Cambridge manuscript of Trevisa bears 'some remarkable similarities' to the Peterborough Lapidary, and Keiser suggests that the differences between the two texts arose only 'perhaps because these entered the Cambridge text at a later stage in the development of its text'.[31]

---

[26] Keiser (1984), pp. xvi–xvii.

[27] Ibid., p. xviii.

[28] Keiser (1992), pp. 344–5. Keiser notes the similarity of the words used in the Peterborough Lapidary, 'strakyd with red strakys', to Bodleian MS e musaeo 16, which has 'with with strakes of red'.

[29] Ibid., p. 345.

[30] Ibid., p. 346. This is not a particularly surprising confusion, given that there is no letter 'v' in gothic script and the letters 'n' and 'u' are virtually indistinguishable.

[31] Ibid., pp. 347–8.

Keiser summarised the state of our knowledge of the sources of the Peterborough Lapidary, which remains incomplete:

> ... the list of sources for the Peterborough Lapidary is probably far more limited than was suggested in [Evans and Serjeantson], for the greater portion of the work comes from one of ... two vernacular sources [the southern *Boke of Stones* and Trevisa's translation of Anglicus]. The compiler incorporates a few scraps from the *De lapidibus* of Marbode of Rennes text and a few others from an unidentified Latin work.[32]

The most interesting feature of the Peterborough Lapidary from a source-critical point of view, is that the lapidarist depended almost entirely on vernacular sources and had access to 'a now lost version of the Anglo-Norman Prose Lapidary'.[33] Keiser promised a much fuller treatment of the Peterborough Lapidary in a forthcoming edition of English prose lapidaries to be published by Garland Press in 1993,[34] but unfortunately this book never materialised.

The manuscript

The Peterborough Lapidary is an unspectacular workaday fifteenth-century manuscript, densely written in two columns in a plain secretary hand across 16 paper folios of 28.5 by 19.5cm.[35] There are generous ruled margins throughout of between 3.5 and 5.8cm in width, but no signs of later annotation. The classmark 'Peterborough Cathedral Library 33', in an early modern italic hand of the late seventeenth or early eighteenth century, is written at the top of fol. 1r. This classmark from Peterborough Cathedral Library (which remains the manuscript's classmark in Cambridge University Library today) refers not just to the Peterborough Lapidary but also to the other material bound together with it. Since the italic classmark probably dates from White Kennett's thorough re-organisation of Peterborough Cathedral Library after 1708, the other material in MS Peterborough Cathedral 33 was presumably bound together with the Peterborough Lapidary in or before the early eighteenth century.

---

[32] Ibid., p. 348.
[33] Ibid.
[34] Ibid., pp. 343–4.
[35] Fols 17–20 are blank, but the margins are ruled in the same way as the rest of the manuscript, suggesting that the compiler prepared them but never wrote on them; fol. 17 is parchment, suggesting that the compiler was short of materials and used anything that came to hand.

According to Evans and Serjeantson's linguistic analysis of the Peterborough Lapidary, 'The language seems to be that of London of the fifteenth century, with few remarkable features', and they were content to designate the manuscript as 'late fifteenth century'.[36] Keiser believed that the Newberry manuscript of Þe Boke of Stones (c. 1430) and the Peterborough Lapidary depended on a common source, and argued that the Newberry manuscript was probably written in Northamptonshire.[37] This raises the possibility that the common source of both manuscripts also originated in Northamptonshire, of which Peterborough was then considered part. The Northamptonshire dialectal features of the Newberry manuscript and the presence of the Peterborough Lapidary in Peterborough Cathedral Library could be explained by both manuscripts having been copied at Peterborough Abbey, one by a local scribe and the other by a Londoner.

There is no record of the library of Peterborough Cathedral acquiring the Peterborough Lapidary after the dissolution, although this does not of course demonstrate that such an acquisition did not occur. Peterborough Cathedral 33 was catalogued as 'Materia Medica, etc.' when loaned to Cambridge University Library in 1970, and that description probably reflected the identifications of earlier librarians. The other material in the manuscript includes an alphabetical list of stones and their synonymous herbs in Latin and Middle English entitled *Albula Argiofara Gemma* (fols 21r–70v); a Latin antidotarium (fols 71r–111r); and a collection of miscellaneous recipes in Latin and English (fols 118r–124r). Whilst it is by no means impossible that a post-Reformation canon of Peterborough Cathedral might have been interested in such a collection, English Benedictine monks were renowned for their medical interests in the late Middle Ages and beyond. Not all manuscripts owned by medieval monasteries, especially in the late Middle Ages, were produced there, and books owned by monks at the time of their profession would find their way into the monastic library. Even if the Peterborough Lapidary was not compiled by a monk of Peterborough, it may have belonged to one – perhaps the infirmarian, charged with looking after the health of the other monks.

---

[36] Evans and Serjeantson (1933), p. 10.
[37] Keiser (1984), p. xi.

Fig. 2. White Kennett (1660–1728), Dean (1707–18) and then Bishop (1718–28) of Peterborough, who reassembled Peterborough Cathedral's library in the early eighteenth century.

Other monastic libraries contained lapidaries long before the compilation of the Peterborough Lapidary in the late fifteenth century. Adam, subprior of St Augustine's, Canterbury, acquired three lapidaries in the early thirteenth century.[38] Unfortunately, a gap in the records of Peterborough's medieval library makes it impossible to confirm whether the lapidary was or was not present there before the dissolution; the last surviving medieval Peterborough catalogue, the *Matricularium*, dates from the late fourteenth century. However, Peterborough was a special case of continuity amongst English Benedictine abbeys because its last abbot, John Chambers, became the first bishop of a newly erected see in 1541, with the old abbey church as his cathedral. Not only that, but Chambers was even appointed warden of the minster in the interim between the dissolution of the abbey and the erection of the see.[39]

At Peterborough there was no demolition of conventual buildings at the time of the dissolution, and even the old abbot's palace survived as the new bishop's palace. As Karsten Friis-Jensen and James Willoughby observe, 'The continuity of personnel from abbey to cathedral offers the hope that the book collection benefited from a measure of institutional stability'. Indeed, many of the monks who had donated books to the monastic library were now canons and prebendaries of the new cathedral and took the opportunity to write their names inside the books. On 31 October 1549 the Dean and Chapter paid 16d to William Ledam, a locksmith, for two locks and keys for the library, and two women were paid to clean the library after some work by stonemasons. According to Friis-Jensen, 'The old monastic book collection ... was transferred to a chamber above the little dorter, a small complex on a limb to the south of the cloister behind the old refectory'.[40] This is shown by a lease of 1585. However, on 22 April 1643, while quartered in Peterborough for the siege of Crowland, Oliver Cromwell's Parliamentarian soldiers ransacked and defaced the cathedral, as well as stealing books; one medieval manuscript which the cathedral clergy had attempted to hide in a wall, the Swaffham Register, had to be bought back from the soldiers for ten shillings.[41] Later the same year Parliament ordered the demolition of

---

[38] Page (2013), p. 10.

[39] Friis-Jensen, K. and Willoughby, J. M. W. (eds), *Peterborough Abbey*, Corpus of British Medieval Library Catalogues 8 (London: British Academy, 2001), p. xxxiv.

[40] Ibid., p. xxxvi.

[41] Ibid., pp. xxxviii–ix.

the cloister arcade, thereby destroying the site of the post-dissolution library.[42]

It seems that many of the books and archives of the cathedral were taken away for the duration of the Interregnum, and the library remained in a state of disorder after the Restoration. Finally, in 1672, the cathedral library was relocated to the fan-vaulted retrochoir (known as the 'New Building'). The celebrated antiquary White Kennett, Dean (1708–18) and then Bishop of Peterborough (1718–28) made strenuous efforts to recover books alienated from the library. Then, in 1780, the library was moved to the first-storey chapel over the west door.[43] At long last, in 1970, the Peterborough Lapidary (along with the rest of the books and manuscripts in Peterborough Cathedral Library pre-dating 1801) was placed on long-term deposit at Cambridge University Library, although the manuscript is still owned by the Dean and Chapter of Peterborough Cathedral.[44]

It is impossible to be certain that the Peterborough Lapidary was ever in Peterborough's medieval monastic library, thanks to there being no fifteenth- or sixteenth-century catalogue of that library. However, rather like the survival of the *Matricularium*, the Peterborough Lapidary's survival of dissolution and Civil War could be attributed to the fact that 'it would have been little regarded for itself and presumably passed unnoticed'.[45] The ire of Cromwell's soldiers was directed against large bound manuscripts that looked like Catholic service books and sealed documents that looked like papal bulls; the Peterborough Lapidary was no more than a few sheets of densely written paper. The London dialect detected by Evans and Serjeantson may simply mean that the compiler of the lapidary – or perhaps the monk who brought it to the monastery – was London-born, and circumstantial evidence supports the idea that the manuscript was in the medieval library of Peterborough Abbey. Benedictine interest in medicine, combined with the fact that the lapidary shared a common source with a manuscript produced in Northamptonshire, the absence of evidence for a post-medieval acquisition and the lack of a fifteenth-century library catalogue, all swing the balance of probability in favour of the manuscript's presence in medieval Peterborough.

---

[42] Ibid., p. xxxvin.

[43] Ibid., pp. xli–ii.

[44] Dourish, E. and Hale, W., 'Incunabula on the Increase: the development of Cambridge University Library's incunabula collections after 1954', *Transactions of the Cambridge Bibliographical Society* 15:1 (2012), pp. 165–74, at pp. 168–9.

[45] Friis-Jensen and Willoughby (2001), p. xxxvi.

Fig. 3. The chapel above the West Porch of Peterborough Cathedral was the site of the Cathedral Library between 1780 and 1970. Photograph by the editor.

Medieval science

It would be a mistake (as well as anachronistic) to adopt a reductive approach to lapidaries, picking out their recognisably 'scientific' content and treating them as early yet clumsy attempts at modern geology, mineralogy or medicine. In the 1960s, the historian of science

R. J. Forbes dismissed the lapidaries as 'an account of the follies and fancies of mankind rather than the tracing of the slow accumulation of scientific data and theories'.[46] Many of the stones that feature in the Peterborough Lapidary are mythical and cannot be identified with any mineral existing in the real world, since in the Middle Ages 'The actual, physical existence of objects took second place to their allegorical existence in a society primarily concerned with the meaning of things'.[47] However, texts such as the Peterborough Lapidary should be read as much for their cultural significance as for the light they may shed on the state of 'scientific' knowledge in fifteenth-century England.

The word 'science' – a nineteenth-century coinage – is itself an anachronism when applied to medieval thought, primarily because medieval speculation about the natural world took place within an Aristotelian framework in which ancient authority carried the same weight as contemporary observation. Medieval people might 'experiment' – carry out certain actions to see what happened – but there was no 'scientific method' in the modern sense of a coherent methodology enabling people to make sense of the results of experiments. Experimental evidence was anecdotal evidence, whose chances of being believed by others depended to a large extent on the perceived authority of the experimenter or reporter. If something was asserted to be true by Aristotle, Theophrastus or Pliny, there was no point testing a statement founded on ancient authority. Nevertheless, the compiler of the Peterborough Lapidary was genuinely interested in how stones came into being and in their observable, testable physical properties as well as in their rumoured occult virtues.

Although the Peterborough Lapidary is the longest and most comprehensive of English lapidaries in terms of the number of stones included, the quality of the text does not compare favourably with some medieval lapidaries. As has already been noted, several stones in the lapidary are repeated in more than one entry, although not always under the same Middle English name. Aetites and celidony occur three times; diamond, jacinth, cinaedia, toadstone, thunderstone, diadochus, dionisius, emerald, liparea, sapphire, serpentine and onyx all appear twice. Clearly, the compiler of the Peterborough Lapidary did not notice that stones with slightly different names in the sources he consulted were actually one and the same. Furthermore, the uncritical attitude of the compiler is revealed in the frequent repetition of the

---

[46] Forbes, R. J., *Studies in Ancient Technology* (Leiden: Brill, 1966), vol. 7, pp. 240–1.
[47] Walton (2001), p. 379.

same stories and virtues within the same entry (described by Keiser as the compiler's 'careless nonsense'[48]). The compiler never seems willing to challenge the authority of his sources, and the furthest he is prepared to go is in his discussion of crystal, in which he seems unconvinced by the theory that crystal is highly compressed ice, and remarks that 'there are many contrary opinions that it is not of great coldness' (p. 23).

Fig. 4: A sixth-century Anglo-Saxon crystal ball pendant, possibly used for divination or as an amulet, excavated at Kempston, Bedfordshire © The British Museum.

---

[48] Keiser (1992), p. 347.

Riddle noted that 'hardly any two lapidaries among the many hundreds are alike', and concluded that 'it is obvious that the compiler of a lapidary exercised personal judgment of some kind in determining what to put in his particular text'.[49] This is certainly true of the Peterborough lapidarist's selection of material, which is not identical to any other known lapidary. The instinct of medieval editors was usually to add new material without subtracting the old, even when new material contradicted what was already there. However, there is also some internal evidence to suggest that even if the compiler did not adopt a particularly critical approach to his sources, he did have some capacity to evaluate and make use of first-hand evidence. For instance, in his discussion of the stone enhydro, the compiler offers his own solution to the problem of how the stone 'sweats' without growing any smaller in size:

> For if the drops were of the substance of the welling stone, why does the stone not become smaller and melt away, if a thing decreases and does not make up for the thing that goes out? But it seems to me that it may be that the virtue of the stone condenses the air that is near it, and turns it into water, and so it seems that it comes out of the stone; however, it comes out of the substance of the air that is around the stone (p. 44).

The compiler's proposed solution – that the liquid 'sweating' from the stone is actually condensation from the air around it – is an eminently sensible suggestion (although it happens to be incorrect). On another occasion, when describing the virtues of sapphire, the compiler mentions an experiment by which a spider can be killed just by placing it in a box close to a sapphire, and claims that 'the same I have tried often in many different places' (p. 67). Although the compiler makes only one explicit reference to 'experyinneces' (experiments), in the context of Circe's mastery of the magic of magnets (p. 62), he frequently exhorts the reader to 'prove' stones, by rubbing them on the tongue, placing them in fire or boiling water, or by other means. He makes several references to stones that have the power to 'draw straws' to them when rubbed vigorously, which may have derived from first-hand experience of electrostatic properties as well as hearsay. On the other hand, since so many of the stones described in the lapidary are not real stones or minerals at all but rather mythical, the compiler cannot have applied any consistent standards of validation.

---

[49] Riddle (1970), p. 50.

The compiler of the Peterborough Lapidary had an active interest in how stones came to be, and many of the descriptions contain an account of a stone's origin. The prevailing assumption in the text, alien in the extreme to modern geology, is that stones are in some sense living beings which can conceive and give birth to other stones. Although some stones are given non-biological origins (such as crystal, formed from compressed ice), most are either of direct biological origin (they are found inside or are made by the bodies of animals) or they behave in a semi-biological fashion. For instance, sapphire is said to be the 'mother' of carbuncle, 'for many men say that the carbuncle is born in the sapphire's veins' (p. 66), and stones are ascribed genders, such as male and female diamond, female paeanite and male and female aetites. The gendering of stones may be reflected in the use of gendered pronouns by the compiler, which is retained in this translation in order to avoid losing an important aspect of the text. The Peterborough lapidarist's attitude towards stones reflects a broader 'vitalism' in medieval natural philosophy, which often saw the universe itself as ensouled (the 'World Soul') as well as individual natural objects within it.[50] Walton observes that 'Developed as a natural extension from the plant and animal world, the gendering of inorganic matter both derived from and at the same time explained observable differences in multiple samples of a single substance'.[51]

The influence of the lapidaries was not confined to the Middle Ages, and lingered even into the Age of Enlightenment. However, Walton has argued that, as time went on, 'lapidary collections ceased to be literary accretions of knowledge and became instead (or at least more so) material accretions'. Physical collections of stones made by wealthy individuals eclipsed the literary lapidary and, in the process, those stones whose existence was solely textual – founded on the authority of the ancients rather than observation – fell into obscurity.[52] The wisdom of the lapidarists became the burgeoning science of mineralogy. However, the switch was far from instantaneous. The sceptical philosopher Francis Bacon (1561–1626) still insisted that 'many things … work upon the spirits of man by secret sympathy and antipathy … [like] the virtues of precious stones … [that] have in them

---

[50] Marsilio Ficino, in spite of his enthusiastic advocacy of the World Soul, rejected the idea that stones generate other stones on the grounds that 'their hard, dense matter occludes the productive spirit in them' (Copenhaver, B. P., *Magic in Western Culture: From Antiquity to the Enlightenment* (Cambridge: Cambridge University Press, 2015), p. 254).

[51] On gendering of stones in medieval sources see Walton (2001), pp. 365–7.

[52] Walton (2001), p. 378.

fine spirits'.[53] John Locke (1632–1704) denounced the snake-stone as 'for the most part if not wholly factitious and of noe … virtue', yet declared his intention to experiment on a bezoar 'which is truly orientall and not counterfeit' – suggesting he did not rule out the possibility of the stone having real properties.[54]

Locke saw no contradiction between accepting Newton's force of gravity – which was then still understood by many to be an 'occult quality' – and believing in the occult forces acting at a distance between herbs, stones and human beings described in the herbals, lapidaries and astrological treatises that remained popular in the seventeenth century. Robert Boyle (1627–91), the father of modern chemistry, sought to explain the electrostatic properties of 'amber, jet and other electricall concretes' in terms of invisible 'effluvia' issuing from the stones.[55] Indeed, the first experimental investigations into electricity examined the electrostatic properties of stones and glass. It was the lapidaries that had kept alive an interest in electrostatic properties throughout the Middle Ages, thereby enabling the discovery of electricity in the Age of Enlightenment.

Medicine in the Peterborough Lapidary

Riddle identified several characteristics of medical, as opposed to Christian and magical lapidaries: 'enlightened usage' of stones (remedies that might actually be effective), description of stones in the form of prescriptions, marginalia indicating that lapidaries were used practically, signatures of known physicians as owners, the appearance of lapidaries in collections of other medical texts, and the cross-referencing of lapidary and herbal knowledge in the text.[56] The Peterborough Lapidary fulfils some of these conditions: many of the stones are described in terms of prescriptive usage for medical complaints, the lapidary appears in the same collection as an antidotarium (treatise on antidotes to poisons), and there are several references to herbs working alongside stones.

---

[53] Quoted in Copenhaver (2015), p. 357.
[54] Ibid., pp. 412–13.
[55] Ibid., p. 404.
[56] Riddle (1970), pp. 40–2.

Fig. 5: Apothecary's jar for storing fragments of emerald (*Frag[menta] Smarag[i]*), c. 1700 © Wellcome Images.

Whilst it would be an exaggeration to describe the Peterborough Lapidary as a medical lapidary, since many of the stones are ascribed no medicinal properties, medicine is one of the main concerns of the compiler; medical conditions are mentioned in around one third of the entries.[57] The Peterborough Lapidary mentions at least 48 medical complaints, not all of them by name, which are identified in the table below (excluding stones said to remove parasites, promote or prevent conception, or aid childbearing, breastfeeding and erectile function).

Table 1: Stones with medical applications in the Peterborough Lapidary

Illness	Stones	Illness	Stones
Ague	6	Hair loss	107
Arthritis	82	Headache	108
Bladder stone	133	Heart disease	108, 114
Blindness	69, 115	Hiccoughs	25
Blisters	41	Impetigo	54
Boils	108	Impostumes	108, 133
Cataracts	115, 136	Infection	69
Colic	15, 39	Jaundice	69, 104
Cramp	41	Kidney disease	52, 115
Dropsy	45, 93, 107, 108, 133	Kidney stones	132, 133
Eczema	54	Liver disease	25
Epilepsy	95	Lunacy	40, 113
Eye complaints	25, 40, 41, 56, 80, 95, 104, 108, 109, 115, 122, 133, 136	Melancholy	96, 108, 116
Falling sickness	70, 107, 109	Menstruation	50, 83, 93, 104
Fever (intermittent, quartan, quotidian, tertian)	15, 40, 56, 93, 109, 128	Murrain	122
Flatulence	108	Nosebleeds	108
Foul evil	4, 6, 41, 83	Obesity	133
Gangrene	69	Palsy	65, 78, 107
Glanders	83	Quinsy	95
Gout	5, 68, 78, 80, 83, 104, 115	Rheum	49

---

[57] 44 of the 145 entries mention medical conditions (30%).

Griping pain	133	Scabies	54, 86
Gum disease	107	Stomach complaints	26, 75, 83, 104, 115, 125, 133
Haemorrhage (bloody flux)	6, 41, 65, 83, 104, 108, 114	Swellings	8, 83, 108, 133
Haemorrhoids	113	Tisic	51

No less than thirteen of the Peterborough Lapidary's medicinal stones are said to help eye complaints, more than any other illness, and this is to be expected given medieval presuppositions about how stones usually transferred their virtues. In the natural philosophy of the period, stones were thought to emit rays or beams that interacted with the beams emitted by the eyes which enabled sight, an idea associated with the Muslim philosopher Al Kindi.[58]

In most cases, the compiler advises that the efficacy of a stone derives just from its being carried by the sick person, although he sometimes recommends grinding up the stone and consuming it with water, wine, milk or honey. The only stone that the compiler recommends burning as a suffumigation is jet (p. 47). In common with recipe collections and, indeed, magical texts of the period, reproductive medicine is a major concern of the compiler. Many stones are said to promote the chances of conception and protect women during pregnancy and childbirth; some are said to ensure an easier labour, and many are associated with increased lactation. Hepatite and niger are said to cure impotence, while magnet is supposed to act as a contraceptive.

Magic in the Peterborough Lapidary

In the Middle Ages lapidaries were never considered to be as dangerous as books of necromancy (ritual magic), designed to call up the devil to do the magician's bidding. Yet, at the same time, lapidaries contained a great deal of information on how to perform magic. In one sense, most medieval thought about the natural world was 'magical thinking' by the standards of contemporary science, and therefore distinguishing 'magic' from 'non-magic' in medieval physical treatises is well-nigh impossible in an absolute sense. However, medieval people had their own standards (albeit imprecise and fluctuating) concerning what might

---

[58] Copenhaver (2015), p. 255.

Fig. 6: Apothecary's jar for storing fragments of sapphire (*L[APIS] SAPHIRVS*), made for the Monastery of El Escorial, Madrid, 1600–1625 © Wellcome Images.

be considered a legitimate exploitation of the hidden properties of nature, given by God, and what might be considered a transgression of God's laws. For instance, the theologian William of Auvergne (d. 1249) argued that it was not possible for stones to impart 'qualities superior to themselves' and therefore they could have no spiritual power over human beings – by giving courage, increasing memory or inciting love.[59] Yet the lapidaries did not hesitate to make such claims, and in doing so they became magical texts.

The ambiguous position occupied by lapidaries in the medieval world, as texts of natural magic, has been well described by Sophie Page:

> While not explicitly magical, lapidaries could encourage readers to exploit the occult powers in natural objects. Marbod of Rennes's popular lapidary ... for example, reveals a sympathy for occult practices: it discusses the hidden mysteries of stones but declines to censure magicians' uses of diamonds and sapphires.[60]

Page has shown that, in the early fourteenth century, the Canterbury monk Michael Northgate tried to link the magical properties of stones in his transcription of a lapidary with accounts of miracles of the saints, thereby establishing a 'sympathetic association between natural marvels and miracles'.[61] Northgate also had a strong interest in natural magic, and his use of lapidaries demonstrates that medieval users of lapidaries did not see the magical properties of stones as phenomena isolated from other kinds of wonders. On the other hand, 'Lapidaries were often primarily orthodox (such as those focussing on the symbolism of the foundation stones of the heavenly Jerusalem) and contained little in the way of explicit practical instructions'.[62] In this way they differed from instruction manuals on how to draw down power from the stars through the creation of images (natural or astrological magic) and, worse still, books of necromantic ritual (grimoires). However, the distinction was not always clear-cut, and 'In practice it is hard to identify purely natural magical operations, because even texts on the virtues of natural objects, such as lapidaries, tended to include some ritual elements to increase their effectiveness'.[63]

---

[59] Page (2013), p. 46.
[60] Ibid., p. 11.
[61] Ibid., p. 19.
[62] Ibid., p. 23.
[63] Ibid., p. 33.

Brian Copenhaver notes that Renaissance magicians made a distinction between stones, amulets and talismans. Stones were 'any small bits of hard mineral', which medieval physicians and apothecaries often prescribed as something to be ground up and consumed as 'an ordinary drug like any other'.[64] The Theory of the Humours, universally held in medieval medicine, meant that as far as physicians were concerned there was no mystery about how ingested minerals acted on the body; their intrinsic virtues acted on the humours, readjusted them and (hopefully) healed the patient. However, a plain stone worn on the body and not ingested could be regarded as an amulet whose causal efficacy was quite literally occult (hidden), since it was not clear how a stone outside the body acted on it. Yet some suffered from conditions that only the power of stones could alleviate, and the church could hardly withhold from the faithful the benefits implanted by God within nature. The canon lawyer William Lyndwood (1417–c. 1429) solved the problem by arguing that someone troubled by evil spirits could carry stones and herbs on his person, provided he did not also seek help from magical incantations.[65]

For the Italian humanist Marsilio Ficino (1433–99), the efficacy of stones worn on the body was due to their correspondence to planets – in other words, it was astrological natural magic: 'These minerals were formed deep within the earth by heavenly power, which stays with them and keeps them connected to the heavens'.[66] Yet, as Copenhaver observes, 'others saw demons lurking behind objects used by godless heathens to protect themselves from disease and devils. Even in all innocence and with the best intentions, wearing an amulet might invite a demon to invade the body of the person wearing it'.[67] To engrave a stone with an image was to take a step further into forbidden territory by creating a talisman – designed, in Ficino's view, to attract celestial virtues, but in the view of his critics designed to attract demonic attention.

Although written at around the same time as Renaissance humanists like Ficino were developing elaborate theories of natural magic, the Peterborough Lapidary remains firmly grounded in the Middle Ages and shows no obvious signs of Renaissance influence. As in Page's 'orthodox' lapidaries, scriptural material – such as the stones

---

[64] Copenhaver (2015), p. 244.

[65] Kelly, H. A., 'Canon Law and Chaucer on Licit and Illicit Magic', in Karras, R. M., Kaye, J. and Matter, E. A. (eds), *Law and the Illicit in Medieval Europe* (Philadelphia, PA: University of Pennsylvania Press, 2008), pp. 210–21, at pp. 212–13.

[66] Copenhaver (2015), p. 243.

[67] Ibid., p. 244.

of the heavenly city in Revelation and the stones set by Moses in Aaron's breastplate – remains quite central to the Peterborough Lapidary. However, 'sympathy for occult practices' is discernible too. Following Marbod's *Liber lapidum*, the Peterborough Lapidary does not censure magical practice, although it suggests that some stones will protect the bearer against harmful magic. Capnite 'will defend ... from wicked enchantments' (p. 27), yet magicians' use of magnets is presented as a recommendation: '[Telemus] the enchanter used it much, for he knew well that it helped much for enchantments; and after him the marvellous enchanter Circe, who was a woman, used it much' (p. 62). Likewise, 'a magus' is the authority for the claim that adredamia 'may be able to settle willing minds' (p. 13).

The Peterborough Lapidary's attitude to witchcraft is similarly ambiguous. The Lapidary contains advice on counter-witchcraft, yet at the same time the practice of witches is appealed to as an authority for the occult properties of some stones. We are told that witches use a kind of agate to 'change tempests and dry up rivers and streams, as it is said' (p. 4), and 'witches' are given as the authority for the claim that pyrite 'refines hastiness and wrath of hearts' (p. 15). We are told of magnets that 'witches use this stone very much' (p. 63). Witches are likewise the authority for coral's resistance to lightning (p. 25). Bloodstone, on the other hand, has a role to play in counter-witchcraft, since the stone 'discerns the folly of enchantments, and of witches who enjoy the pride of their own wonders, by which they beguile men with the wonders they work' (p. 41). Likewise, jet 'prevents witchcraft and charms' (p. 47) and sardine 'preserves his bearer from enchantments and from witchcraft' (p. 71). Sapphire seems to act both against and for witches: 'the sapphire is very good ... to break witchcraft', yet 'witches love this stone especially well, for they believe that they do certain wonders by the virtue of this stone' (p. 65).

Perhaps even more striking than the Lapidary's ambivalence towards witchcraft is its failure to condemn explicitly necromantic practices. We are assured that 'Those who use necromancy say that they are more able to have answer of God and are more heard by the sapphire than by other precious stones' (p. 67). Onyx 'allows a man to speak to his dead friend by night in a meeting' (p. 90), while diadochus makes a dead body move, 'And if you want, you may command whichever devil of hell you want and the devil will do no man harm' (p. 37). Likewise, the bearer of anancite 'may command the devil to you, and he will obey you whatever you want to say, and he will do you no harm' (p. 13). The method prescribed for obtaining the toadstone is almost identical to an 'experiment', found in many grimoires, for obtaining bones from a toad for use in divination: 'take the toad and put him in a new earthenware pot, and make many holes in it, and put it in an ant hill, and cover over the pot; and then the ants will eat all of the toad except the bones, and you will find the stone stuck on the head of the toad' (p. 28).[68]

The Peterborough Lapidary betrays the influence of astrological magic by insisting that certain stones must be set in a specific metal in order to enable or enhance their effectiveness. According to astrological magical theory, herbs, stones and metals corresponded with different planetary influences; combining them (by setting a stone under one planet in a metal under another, for example) allowed the astral magician to manipulate heavenly forces on earth. So, for instance, we are told that diamond, toadstone, jacinth, topaz and ruby must be set in gold. We are informed concerning jasper that 'his virtue is greater in silver than in gold' (p. 53) and of onyx that 'his virtue is in gold' (pp. 89–90). Serpentine, on the other hand, may be set in either gold or silver (p. 61). Sympathetic magic – the idea that physical resemblance enables magical effectiveness – also features in the Peterborough Lapidary. It is because toadstone, found in the head of the venomous toad, contains a shape like a toad that it is effective as a remedy against poison and venom: 'sometimes the shape of the toad seems to be within it, with broad and shaped feet' (p. 84).

On a closer reading, it is clear that the Peterborough Lapidary not only condones but also enables the conjuration of demons; indeed, it even includes ritual prescriptions of its own. Whoever wants to engrave jasper should do so 'with a sword in his hand, with a stole about his neck and a staff that should be of olive wood' (p. 53). Sword, stole and rod are the standard tools of the ritual magician, signifying authority over spirits.[69] The sword represented the necromancer's power to harm evil spirits by exorcism, the stole the authority of the church (necromancers were often clerics) and the rod stood for the wonderworking staff of Moses.[70] The requirement for the engraver of jasper to be equipped as a ritual magician implies either that the stone

---

[68] On traditions of toad magic see Chumbley, A. D., *The Leaper Between: An Historical Study of the Toad-bone Amulet* (Three Hands Press, 2012), pp. 21, 26–9.

[69] See Harms, D., Clark, J. R. and Peterson, J. H. (eds), *The Book of Oberon: A Sourcebook of Elizabethan Magic* (Woodbury, MN: Llewellyn, 2015), p. 290; Foreman, P., *The Cambridge Book of Magic: A Tudor Necromancer's Manual* (Cambridge: Texts in Early Modern Magic, 2015), pp. 117–19.

[70] On the use of material objects in ritual magic see my forthcoming chapter, Young, F., '*Instruments of nigromancie*: materials of ritual magic in late medieval and early modern England' in Bosselmann-Ruickbie A. and Ruickbie L. (eds), *The Material Culture of Magic* (Leiden: Brill).

was protected by spirits or that engraving the stone was meant to call spirits into it, turning it into a magical talisman.

The Peterborough Lapidary's insistence on the connection between the powers of stones and the spiritual state of their owners also takes it into magical territory. Ritual magicians, like exorcists, believed that the effectiveness of their operations depended on their personal purity and freedom from sin: the sacraments of the church worked automatically (*ex opere operato*) but exorcism and magic worked *ex opere operantis* – 'from the deed of the operator'.[71] The Peterborough Lapidary suggests that, while the power of stones is inherent in their nature, because it derives from God and is holy it can also be diminished by the sins of the bearer. Being out of mortal sin is given as a condition for bearing several stones, although this on its own does not mean that the stones lose their virtue because of sin – it may simply mean that an unworthy bearer would incur divine displeasure. However, we are told that 'He who bears sardine, onyx and chalcedony will be well enriched, unless he loses his virtue through sin' (p. 20). The Lapidary even offers a solution for 're-charging' stones that have lost their virtue on account of sin: 'if any stone has lost his virtue through sin, let a man confess his sin, and take and wash the crystal in pure water and touch the stone with [crystal], and soon he will take his virtue again by the virtue of the crystal' (p. 22).

The Peterborough Lapidary also includes stones with properties enabling divination. If someone 'washes his mouth and holds [a sapphire] under his tongue, as long as the moon is waxing, a man may divine from the morning until midday' (p. 13). Similarly, 'If a man puts [calonite] in his mouth early in the morning until the sixth hour of the waxing of the moon, he may divine all that is to come after' (p. 30). Emerald is likewise recommended for divination, and the Lapidary recounts the story that the Emperor Nero had an emerald mirror in which he saw 'all that he sought or desired' (p. 38). Magical mirrors were staples of medieval necromancy. Although the Peterborough Lapidary never explicitly mentions 'scrying' (the practice of seeing spirits in a crystal), the most famous practitioner of this art, John Dee (1527–1608) turned to the medieval lapidaries in the 1580s to discover which stones attracted good spirits and repelled demons. Dee was working with a scryer, Edward Kelley, but was concerned about the danger of evil spirits masquerading as good ones.[72] There were at least

---

[71] Young, F., *A History of Exorcism in Catholic Christianity* (London: Palgrave MacMillan, 2016), p. 127.
[72] Page (2013), p. 135.

five lapidaries in Dee's extensive library.[73] Protection from spiritual attack is one of the concerns of the Peterborough Lapidary: chalcedony 'helps against tricks and scorns of fiends' (p. 21); coral is useful against 'the fiend's guile' (p. 25); amethyst, collorus and diamond offer help against harm from wicked spirits; and emerald 'helps against all fantasies and japes of fiends' (p. 69).

Dee's annotation of his lapidaries also shows that he was interested in ritual consecrations that would increase the power of stones, for example by placing a stone on the altar so that mass would be said over it.[74] The Peterborough Lapidary contains one such consecration; celidony, the stone found in the womb of a swallow, 'is very valuable if it is held up at the sacrament and is wound in a linen cloth' (p. 24). This is a reference to the elevation or 'sacring', the moment in the mass when the consecrated host was lifted up and shown to the people – a moment suffused with sacred power in late medieval English culture when even those outside the church would drop to their knees on hearing the sacring bell. White linen was associated with purity in books of ritual magic, and the consecration of celidony resembles the consecrations of *lamina* (pieces of metal inscribed with magical sigils) in texts of necromancy.[75]

---

[73] Ibid., p. 210 n. 11.

[74] Ibid., p. 135.

[75] See Foreman (2015), pp. 3, 34, 40, 65, 68, 84, 102, 114.

Fig. 7. A crystal pendant owned by John Dee (1527–1608/9) and possibly used by him for divination © Wellcome Images.

Fig. 8. The lapidary at work, engraving by B. L. Prevost after J. N. F. Boucher (eighteenth century) © Wellcome Images.

EDITOR'S NOTE

Middle English text

The text here printed is an exact transcription of the text of CUL MS Peterborough Cathedral 33, including words reduplicated by the scribe in error. No attempt has been made to retain the original layout of the text. In the original manuscript the stones are neither numbered nor (in most cases) given headings. The numbering of the stones in this edition follows Evans and Serjeantson's edition of 1933, and headings are given in square brackets to indicate that they are editorial additions and do not appear in the original manuscript. Punctuation of the text follows Evans and Serjeantson's edition; the insertion of punctuation into a largely unpunctuated medieval text is always somewhat arbitrary, and there is no reason why the present editor's choices should be better than those of the first editors. However, it is necessary to insert punctuation in order to make clearer the relationship between text and translation.

Readings suggested by Evans and Serjeantson (many of which I have accepted for the sake of the translation) and other scholars are given in the footnotes; my own suggested readings of doubtful words likewise appear in the footnotes. Transcription of the Middle English text follows the use of the letters thorn (Þ, þ) and yogh (ȝ, ȝ) in the original manuscript. Conventional scribal abbreviations are expanded in italics (e.g. ver*tu*); where the scribal abbreviation is lacking the probable missing letter(s) are given in square brackets (e.g. b[l]ak). Insertions in the original text are indicated \thus/ and deletions struck through ~~thus~~. Illegible text is indicated by [*illeg.*].

Translation

The aim of the translation is to produce a readable text in modern English that is as close in meaning and sense to the Middle English original as possible, as well as to render into English the small number of Latin passages in the manuscript. This has primarily involved the grammatical reorganisation of the text and the replacement of archaic vocabulary. Archaic-sounding words and phrases have been avoided in the translation, except where it is absolutely necessary to retain them for the sense of the text. However, the use of gendered pronouns for stones has been retained in the translation as it reflects the compiler's attitude to stones as living beings. In a small number of instances the meaning of the Middle English text is obscure, and in these instances I have rendered the text word for word into modern English in order to leave the passages open to the reader's interpretation.

Unlike Evans and Serjeantson, I have chosen (where possible) in the inserted headings to identify the stones of the Middle English text with their modern English or late Latin equivalents. My justification for this is that it makes it possible to compare the content of the Peterborough Lapidary with other lapidaries and medieval and Classical encyclopaedias. In most cases the identifications derive from Lewis, R. E. (ed.), *Middle English Dictionary* (Ann Arbor, MI: University of Michigan Press, 1952–2001), 118 vols. Identifications of stones are in many cases far from certain, and these should be taken as indicative rather than final.

THE PETERBOROUGH LAPIDARY

[Cambridge University Library MS Peterborough Cathedral 33,
fols 1r–16v]

[Prologue]

[fol. 1r] This is þe boke þat euax kyng of Arabe sent to tyberi off rom, of all maner of precius stones as well as of her names, vertues, as of here colours & her contreys þat þey ben founde ynn, & of the assayi*ng* how3 ye schul know he*m*. Also he seythe that no ma*n* schall be in dowte þat god haþe set & put gret vertu in worde, stone & erbe, by the wyche, if it so be þat men be not of mysbeleue & Also owte of dedly synne, & ma*ny* & owde & full[76] mervailes my3t be wrow3t þorow her vertues. And also he seiþe þat god takeþ stones for a precius tresow*ur*. & therfor I propose to certifey her names folowy*ng* in order*e* heraft*er* by the A b C, boþe of the bok of euax of All þe stones þat sei*nt* Iohne eua*ng*elist & apostell þe which were schewde to hi*m* i*n* heue*n* wen*e* he lay i*n* cristes lape; And also of the stones of Auycene, ysodor, Diascorides, Plyni*us*, Dias, bartholom*us*, Richard ruf*us*, & ma*ny* other þat trete*n* of precious stones. And so to begyne I schall rerese[77] her colours, vertues, co*n*treys & places þat þey co*m* out of.

This is the book that Evax king of Arabia sent to Tiberius of Rome, about all manner of precious stones as well as about their names, virtues, and about their colours and their countries that they are found in, and about the method by which you will know them. Also he says that no man will be in doubt that God has set and put great virtue in word, stone and herb; by which, if men are not errorroneous in belief and also in no mortal sin, many old and true marvels might be wrought through their virtues. And also he says that God takes stones for a precious treasure. And therefore I propose to certify their names following in order hereafter alphabetically, both out of the Book of Evax and of all the stones that St John the Evangelist and Apostle which were shown to him in heaven when he lay in Christ's lap; and also out of the stones of Avicenna, Isidore, Dioscorides, Pliny, Dioscorides, Bartholomaeus Anglicus, Richard Rufus and many others who treat of precious stones. And so to begin I shall rehearse their colours, virtues, countries and places that they come out of.

---

[76] Evans and Serjeantson read 'wonderful'.
[77] Evans and Serjeantson read 'reherse'.

1. [Apsyctos[78]]

Absittus is a stone þat is sum-wat of blac*es* colo*ur*, a partie drawy*n*g to the colo*ur* of red, & he is good evyn wei3t*es* & mesors, & he takeþ het of the fir*e* & so lasteþ xij dayis. Ysidor*e* seyþe þat he is a *precius* stone, blake & hevy & strakyd w*ith* red strakys & red weynes. t° de gemmis, ysidr*e*.

Apsyctos is a stone that is somewhat of blackish colour, a part approaching the colour of red, and he is good even for weights and measures, and he takes heat of the fire and so lasts twelve days. Isidore says that he is a precious stone, black and heavy and streaked with red streaks and red veins (the third book[79] *Of Gems*, Isidore).

2. [Agate]

Achate is a stone fownd i*n* þe orie*n*t in a flom which is cleped achate; & some seyþ þat he cometh owte of cecyl, & ther is founde; & he is of many maner3: þat one is blak & oue*r*girde w*ith* whi3t veynes, & so he haþe al a whi3t crose, & he haþe whi3t figures as of a crosse. Dias. And such þer ben*e* þat haue branchis, figured as trees & as leuys, hedys, þat ky*n*de haþe put to. And some th*er* be*n* grene as of iaspe, dipped w*ith* red droppis; and þis maner of achate is cleped of myche folk Diodropie, þat mych is of v*er*tu & *m*iche yn device of lapidar*ies*. And such Achates þer ben*e* that han gold vey*n*is. Þe script*ur* tellit vs þat þer ben*e* som of colo*ur* of gold & of ense*n*s & of mire & of coral droppid. Þis achat te*m*po*r*eth

Agate is a stone found in the Orient in a river which is called Achates; and some say that he comes out of Sicily, and there is found; and he is of many kinds: one is black and overgirt with white veins, and so he has all a white cross, and he has white figures as of a cross (Dioscorides). And there are such as have branches, figured as trees and as leaves, heads, that kind has put to. And there are some that are as green as jasper, dipped with red spots. And this kind of agate is called by many people Diodropia, and is of much virtue and much used by lapidaries. And there are such agates as have gold veins. The scripture tells us that there are some of the colour of gold, of incense and of myrrh, and of

---

[78] A stone mentioned by Pliny the Elder, unidentifiable with any known mineral.

[79] 't°' can be read either as 't[erti]o' ('in the third') or 'tomo' ('in the book').

softly & comforteþ old men. And þer is an oder colour as coral, he hath gret yoynetes[80] as gold; and anoþer that haþe þe smell of myrre, and anoþer þat haþe colour as wexe. All þe maner of achates ben god aȝens biȝting of serpents & he kepeþ A man fro euell þinges; & he encresite strengþe & makeþ god spekyng togeder & creable & of goode colour; he geueþ gode consayl & he makeþ good beleue, he holpeþ þe blesauns to god & to þe wordell. And he seiþe þat þer is an achat þat is blak & haþe forme of many kyndes, as semeing of kinges or of princes, for suche is his apparacion of your lord þat swet figure; in þis maner is his knowyng. **[fol. 1v]** Also som seyn þat þer is oon & is browȝt owȝt of a contrey lyk to coral, & another lik to wexe of gret valewe.

Also bartholomewe seiþe: accipe lapidem achatem dicitur est niger habens albas venas & iste facit vincere periculam & vires confert cordibus & facit hominem gratum potentem & placentem iocundem & secundum & iuuat contra aduersa.

Also we fynd in redyng of old bokes þat þer is such an achates

spotted coral. This agate tempers softly and comforts old men. And there is another colour, as coral; he has great points of gold; and another that has the smell of myrrh, and another that has the colour of wax. All the kinds of agate are good against the biting of serpents, and he keeps a man from evil things; and he increases strength and makes good speaking together and is creditable and of good colour. He gives good counsel and he makes good belief. He helps the blessings to God and to the world. And he says that there is an agate that is black and has many kinds of forms, seeming to be those of kings and princes, for such is his appearance of your lord, that sweet figure; in this manner is his knowing. Also some say that there is one that is brought out of a country, similar to coral, and another similar to wax of great value.

Also Bartholomaeus says: 'Take a stone named agate; it is black and having white veins; and this will make you defeat danger and unites men in their hearts and makes a man grateful, powerful and pleasing, cheerful and favourable, and helps against adversities'.

Also we find, in reading old books, that there is such an agate

---

[80] Evans and Serjeantson read 'poynctes'.

þat woso put it in an herke[81] þat is clepid þe gold, & put it in his fist close, no man may se hem. As þe bokes seyne, þis maner sueþ þe sone; þis maner of achate is green droppid with red. Moyses put þis achates vpon þe brest of arone his broder, & was blak & had whiȝt branches; & þis stone was set in þe þrid corner of þe brist of arone. Also þer is of anoþer maner of achate which is founde in creta, as diascorides seiþ, & it haþe a blewe weyne. And þer is anoþer kinde, þe which cometh oute of Inde, with red droppis, as ysidore seith. Men trowen þat þe fyst maner þerof helpiþ wich-crafte, for þer-with þei changen tempest & stauncheþ ryvers and stremes, as it is seid.

that whoever puts it in a herb that is called 'the gold', and puts it close in his fist, no man may see him. As the books say, this kind sues the sun; this kind of agate is green spotted with red. Moses put this agate on the breast of Aaron his brother, and it was black and had white branches; and this stone was set in the third corner of the breast of Aaron. Also there is another kind of agate which is found in Crete, as Dioscorides says, and it has a blue vein. And there is another kind which comes out of India, with red spots, as Isidore says. Men say that the fifth kind thereof helps witchcraft, for with it they change tempests and dry up rivers and streams, as it is said.

Also dias seiþe þat þe same kend is gode to schappes & ymages of kinges & to schew lykenes of sclepis;[82] & þe maner kynde of creata changeþ perels, & makeþ graciose, plesyng, & fayr spekyng & shewyng, & yeueþ myȝth & strengþe. Þe maner of ston of ynd com-fort þe liȝt[83] & helpit aȝens wenym, & it smellith swet & it be niȝt, as dias seiþe.

Also Dioscorides says that the same kind is good for shapes and images of kings and to show likeness of shapes; and the Cretan kind changes dangers, and makes for gracious, pleasing and fair speaking and showing, and gives might and strength. The Indian kind of stone comforts the sight and helps against venom, and it smells sweet if it is night, as Dioscorides says.

---

[81] Evans and Serjeantson read 'herbe'.
[82] Evans and Serjeantson read 'schapis'.
[83] Evans and Serjeantson read 'siȝt'.

4

3. [Androdama[84]]

Andromada is a stone of iiij maner liknes, & is lik to siluer, & of hardnes, lik to þe diamaunt; & he is founde in þe red se, & he makeþ a man ys wite to stedefastnes.

Androdama is a stone of three kinds of appearance, and is similar to silver, and in its hardness similar to the diamond; and he is found in the Red Sea, and he makes a man's understanding to be steadfast.

4. [Aetites]

Achites is nombred amonges þe stones þat be good; þe egle sekeþe him in þe vtterist parte of the wordil, & he berith to his nest to defend. Þis ston hath a-noþer ston with-yn him & is moche worthe to wemen with child, þat sche lese not her child; & þey schull ber it in her left side. And a man þat bereth it, he holdeth him in a men statt, & defendiþ oldnes, & he encrecith riches; & he þat beriþ him schall be wolbelouid & avaunsed; & it makeþ a child to encrese & kepiþ his wytt, & helþe & doþe awaye þe fowle euell. And yf a man haue to anoþer suspecion of yuel, do put þis ston vndir þe dische þat he schall ett of, & he schall mow ett no mett til þe ston be done awaye. And þis ston is round, & is fovnde in de gret see of occian; & it is good & helping to men in batail, & kep a man sobre; & som seyne it is found in þe egle nest. See mor of þis ston in Etite.

Aetites is numbered among the stones that are good. The eagle seeks him in the furthest part of the world, and he bears him to his nest to defend. This stone has another stone within him and is much worth to women with child, so that she loses not her child. And she should bear it on her left side. And a man that bears it will hold himself in a mean state and will defend old age, and he will increase riches; and he that bears him shall be well beloved and advanced; and it makes a child increase and keep his understanding, and helps and does away with the foul evil. And if a man has against another suspicion of evil, put this stone under the dish that he shall eat of, and he shall eat no more meat until the stone is taken away. And this stone is round, and is found in the great sea of Ocean;[85] and it is good and helpful to men in battle, and keeps a man sober; and some say it is

---

[84] A kind of bloodstone.
[85] The Atlantic Ocean.

found in the eagle's nest. See more about this stone under Aetites.

5. [Adamas]

Adamas *vel* asius is a ston þat is liȝt in bering, & his colour is witȝt in him [with] b[l]ak tacchis; & hoso will preue him, ley him vpon his tonge & frot hit a litel, & Anon a schall wax whitter þen he was befor. And whosoo berith þis ston scall nat haue þe goute nor be potagre, ne non oþer euel schal fal in his legis; & yf eny yuel comeþ, brek this ston into povder & drink it with wyne, & þen scall be hol.

Adamas or *asius* is a stone that is light in bearing, and his colour is white in him with black spots; and whoever wants to prove him, let him lay him on him on his tongue and rub it a little, and soon it will become whiter than he was before. And whoever bears this stone will not have the gout nor be podagrous, nor will any other evil befall his legs; and if any evil comes, break this stone into powder and drink it with wine, and then you shall be whole.

[fol. 2r] Require vlterius in diamonde.

Search elsewhere under diamond.

6. [Diamond]

Adamant is a ston of his name, þat no man may be ouer-come when a man bereþ it vpon him. And all-so ley it vpone an Andefeld of yrene or of stell, & smyte þer vpone with a gret hamer of yrene, for [more] is apeired þe hamer & þe anfeld þen is þe ston, & so a man may preve & þe adamant be worþ or no. And þow it be so þat a man may by no engenns of yrun brek it, in hot new blod of a gote boke & it will in schort tyme breke & departe into many parties. And also þes vertues it haþe, þat hoso berith it vpone him dar not not

Diamond is a stone of his name, and no man may be overcome when he bears it upon him. And also lay it on an anvil of iron or of steel, and strike it with a great hammer of iron, and the hammer and the anvil will be more damaged than the stone; and so a man may prove whether the diamond is valuable or not. And although a man may by no engines of iron break it, put it in the hot new blood of a goat and it will in a short time break and part it into many pieces. And also it has these virtues, that whoever dred of þe blody flyx ne of þe fowle agewe, ne no þefes schal tak hi*m*, ne he schall not fale i*n* no such greua*n*ce ne harme. And he þ*at* bereth it schal not be ouer-come i*n* bataile. Also a ma*n* must close hi*m* in golde, & he most ber hi*m* on his lefte honed & while þ*u* berist & be owte of dedly synne þ*er* schal no wikkid spret ~~be~~ ne enfy of ma*n*ky*n*d do þe harme þ*er* as þe adama*n*t ȝeueþ lyȝt, ne he schall dey sclepyng, ne no pride oue*r*come hi*m*, ne evel swendes schall hant hi*m*; & þ*u* schal be curtes & loue goddes seruyse; & it schall defe*n*d þe of þi*n* ene*m*ye. Lok þ*u* do no dedly synn*e* while þ*u* hast þ*is* adama*n*t vpone þe. Þ*is* preved euax kyng of araby & oþ*er* many mo.

bears it upon him will dare not dread the bloody flux nor the foul ague, nor shall any thieves take him, nor shall he fall into any grievance or harm. And he who bears it shall not be overcome in battle. Also a man must enclose him in gold, and he must bear him on his left hand, and while you bear it and are out of mortal sin, no wicked spirit nor envy of mankind will do you harm there, as the diamond gives light, nor will he die sleeping, nor will pride overcome him, nor will evil dreams haunt him; and you will be courteous and love God's service; and it will defend you from your enemy. Look that you do no mortal sin while you have this diamond upon you. This proved Evax king of Arabia and many others more.

Require vlt*er*ius i*n* magnet*es*.

See elsewhere under magnet.

7. [Agapis]

Agatten is a ston*e*, & it is lik þe skyn of a lion. Som*e* clepiþ it agapis. Yf a ma*n* be wou*n*ded w*ith* eny egge tole w*ith* þe poynte, tak þ*at* ston*e* agaten*e* & wassh hi*m* i*n* clene wat*er*, & þen ley it to þe wou*n*de, & it schall draue by þe v*er*tu of þis ston all þe wenem owte of þe wou*n*de. And if eny scorpio*n* or eny serpent sty*n*ge eny best, mak þ*is* ston to powder & ley it opon*e* þe wou*n*de or dri*n*ke it w*ith* with wiȝt wyne, & þey sall be hol. Wyles þ*u* berest þe stone

Agapis is a stone that is like the skin of a lion. Some call it agapis. If a man is wounded with any edged tool with a point, take that stone agapis and wash him in clean water, and then lay it on the wound, and it will draw by the virtue of this stone all the venom out of the wound. And if any scorpion or any serpent stings any beast, make this stone to powder and lay it on the wound or drink it with white wine, and they will be whole. While you bear this stone

7

þu schal loue goddys servise; þis preuede þe emperour Tiberius.

you will love God's service; this proved the emperor Tiberius.

8. [Alectorius]

Alistores *vel* alettoria is a ston whiȝt shynynge lik to crystal water þu schald fynd him onder An old cok or vnder an old capene; wene þey ben passed vij yer old þey will gendir þis stone in her wombe, & þis stone is clepid alistores. Þese ben his vertues: he þat berith þis ston vpone him, he schal be hardy on his enemyes; he þat bereþ ouer his helme, he schale neuer be discomfet in werre.

Alectorius is a stone white shining, similar to crystal water. You will find him under an old cock or under an old capon. When they have passed seven years old they will produce this stone in their womb, and this stone is called alectorius. These are his virtues: he who bears this stone upon him, he will be resolute against his enemies; he who bears it over his helmet will never be discomforted in war.

Also dias seiþ, who-so berith þis stone he schal be a coriquerour. Also who-so bereþ þis stone vpone, he schall be lecherowse & amarowse of wommen, & a fayr speker. And yf he haue eny opostume in his body, mak powder of þis stone & drinke it, & he schall be hole; þis preued croantis[86] in battaile.

Also Dioscorides says that whoever bears this stone will be a conqueror. Also whoever bears this stone on him will be lecherous and amorous of women, and a fair speaker. And if he has any swelling in his body, make powder of this stone and drink it, and he will be whole; this proved Milo of Croton in battle.

Some men seyn þat þis stone groweth fro iij ȝer age til he be vij ȝer old, & it is founde in þe capons wombe; & it is lyke trobel cristall. And yf a man haue gret þurst, put þis ston in his mouþe & it schal help him anon. Also a man or womman may not conceyue, ber þis stone vpone him & þey

Some men say that this stone grows from three years of age until he is seven years old, and it is found in the capon's womb; and it is like cloudy crystal. And if a man has great thirst, put this stone in his mouth and it will soon help him. Also if a man or woman cannot conceive, let him bear this

---

[86] Duffin (2007b), p. 335 reads 'croantis' as a corruption of 'Crotonis', i.e. a reference to Milo of Croton.

shal conceyue anoon. And it is godd for a woman þat will have of her lord or of her master. Also þis ston makeþ a woman to be delyuerd [of] child & encresþ well mylk, so it be used before m[*off edge of page*].[87]

stone upon him and they will soon conceive. And it is good for a woman who wants something of her lord or of her master. Also this stone makes a woman to be delivered of her child and increases milk well, so it is used before …

[fol. 2v] Also many kynges han had þe victorie in battail & it helpiȝt myche in cases. And he schall be gracius þat bereþ. Also dias seyþe þat þis stone excitþ þe seruice of venus; & he makeþ a man gracius, & stedfast, & victoriose, & wise, & redy, & connynge in plee, & it acordeth frendes & quencheþ þrist in þe mowthe.

Also many kings have had victory in battle and it helps much in cases. And he will be gracious who bears it. Also Dioscorides says that this stone excites the service of Venus, and he makes a man gracious, and steadfast, and victorious, and wise, and ready, and cunning in plea, and it brings friends into accord and quenches thirst in the mouth.

9. [Alabaster]

Alabastre is a stone þat is cendre & whiȝt when it is grounde. Whoso drinkeþ him with eysel, he is good for all maner sores in þe fote or in þe knee.

Alabaster is a stone that is ash-coloured and white when it is ground. Whoever drinks him with vinegar, then he is good for all manner of sores in the foot or in the knee.

10. [Garnet]

Alabanda is a ston of the kyngdom of Asie; & þis alabanda is myche lyke þe colour of sardayne; & he makeþ scharpnes of iuges. Ysodre seyþ þat þis ston alabanda is a precius ston, cler & comndable rede as sardines; þe vertu þerof exciteþ & echeþ

Garnet is a stone of the kingdom of Asia; and this garnet is much like the colour of sardine; and he makes for sharpness of judges. Isidore says that this stone garnet is a precious stone, clear and commendable, red as sardine; its virtue excites and stimulates the

---

[87] Evans and Serjeantson suggest 'm[ete]'.

blode.

blood.

11. [Alemandine[88]]

Alemandyne comeþ owte of a lonnde þat is clepid dayse, þat [is] clepid asabrace. It resembleþ mych to sardine, þat yvel it is know þe ton fro þe odere.

Alemandine comes out of a land that is called Dacia, that is called Asabracia. It very much resembles sardine, so that it is difficult to know the one from the other.

12. [Spinel]

Alpitistes is a red stone schynyng, & it is of such vertu þat it leteþ þe cawdryn of cedyng or boylyng, & coleþ þe water in schorte time. It doþ away þe briddes of þe londe þat is swet, & it fordoþe med-lynges, & makeþ a man hole; & put it in þe sonne beme & it ȝeueþ briȝtnes as it were feire; and yf þu wolt bere it þu most bere it one þy riȝth side.

Spinel is a shining red stone, and it is of such virtue that it prevents the cauldron from flourishing or boiling, and cools the water in a short time. It does away the sweet birds of the land, and it prevents meddling, and makes a man whole; and put it in the sun beam and it gives brightness as if it were fair; and if you want to bear it you must bear it on your right side.

13. [Asbestos]

Albestus or asbestus is a stone þat comeþ owte of þe contrey of archady. Þis ston haþ coler lik to þe colour of yrene, & it is a wondere kynd, for if he oones liȝth he with-holdeþ mych feyre, & þer may welneȝt no þeng quenche þe lieȝt of him. Þat stone is made with so crafty þinges of which naciouns þey[89] tak with sacrelege wondrede; for in a temple of venus is made a

Asbestos is a stone that comes out of the country of Arcadia. This stone has a colour similar to the colour of iron, and it is of a wondrous kind, for if he is once lit he withholds much fire, and well nigh nothing may quench his light. That stone is made with so many skilful things of which nations they take with wondrous sacrilege; for in a temple of Venus is made a candlestick, one which

---

[88] A type of ruby from the Greek city of Alabanda.
[89] Evans and Serjeantson read 'þ[at]'.

candlestick one þe which was a lantren so brenynge þat it miȝt not be quenched with tempest ne with rayne, as ysodre seiþe, Il° xvj° t° de gemmis.

was a lantern burning in such a way that it could not be quenched neither with tempest nor with rain, as Isidore says, in that sixteenth book *Of Gems*.

14. [Aristinctus]

Aristinctus is a ston riȝt hardy. Yf a man smyteþe one it will flawmy sperkyls as it wer feyre owte of þis stone; & ley it vpone herdis of flex, & [*illeg.*] herdes with þe powder þer as þu art brent, it schal hele þe brennyng; also þu miȝtest smyȝte fir þer-of vpone herdis.

Aristinctus is a very hardy stone. If a man smites one it will flame sparks like fire out of this stone; and lay it upon herds of flocks, and herds with the powder there when you are burnt, it will heal the burning; also you might smite its fire upon herds.

15. [Amethyst]

Amatitus is a ston like to purpull red as [*illeg.*] wyne or red rose in color. Þe boke telleþ vs þat þis ston is comfortable to him þat bereþ it when wild bestees comen to him; & it is mych comfortable in all sorowþ. And it holdeþ a man in gode beleive & stronge boþe to body & to soule to him þat bereþ it worþely & clenly. And whoso bereþ him schall singe clerly & with gode voys. And as þe boke of Moyses tellith þe, he þat bereþ him schall schall be welcome before þe kynges and lordes, & delyuerly he schall worche þe craft þat he entermeteþ of. And it makeþ a man mek. Whoso bereþ þis stone schall haue in him þe more l mynde of god, & be gracious. Also whoso bereþ þis [a]metist no euel spret schal haue pover to don him harme; neiþer he

Amethyst is a stone like purple red, like wine or a red rose in colour. The book tells us that this stone is comforting to him who bears it when wild beasts come to him; and it is very comforting in all sorrows. And it holds a man in good belief and strength both of body and soul to him who bears it worthily and purely. And whoever bears him will sing clearly and with good voice. And as the book of Moses tells you, he that bears him will be welcome before kings and lords, and directly he will work the skill that he undertakes. And it makes a man meek. Whoever bears this stone will be more mindful of God, and be gracious. And whoever bears this amethyst, no evil spirit will have power to do him harm; nor will he have any evil dreaming at night, schal haue no yuel dremyng any3t; neþer in feyre ne in water **[fol. 3r]** neiþer feuer, ne he schal dred; & his catel schall encrese, & his enemy schall neuer ouercome him in a ri3tfull qwarell; neiþer he schall be prisoned ne dy withoute repentauns of his misdedes, ne long be in presoun, but if it be in relegius; ne no horse schall founde vnder him, ne he schall not assent to eny tresoun, neþer horse þat he reyþ[90] one schall neuer haue þe wormes ne trenche. Also isodre seiþe þat amitistus is pupel red in color, & is medeled with þe color of violet, as it were a blasinge rose, & li3tly casting ow[t] as it were schinyng bemes þat 3iuen li3t. Also ysed seyþ þat þer is a-noder kynde which is myche lyke to blow & he is not al fry[91] but he haþe vertu of hete, and þer ben v kendes þer-of as þias seyþ. Also diascorides seiþ þat þe purpel red is most noble & better þen þe oþer, for þe vertu of helpit a3en dronknes, & makeþ a man to worche, & putteþ away ydel þout3tes & maketh gode vnder-stondyng; & it is nessh, so þat mene may graue þeryne & writhe. Of þis color schul kynges cloþe hem when þei holden her courtes.

neither in fire nor in water, nor fever, nor will he fear; and his cattle will increase, and his enemy will not overcome him in a rightful quarrel; nor will he be imprisoned nor die without repentance of his misdeeds, nor be long in prison, unless it is a religious one; nor will any horse stumble under him, nor will he assent to any treason, and no horse that he rides will ever have the worms or colic. Also Isidore says that amethyst is purple red in colour, and is mixed with the colour of violet, as it were a blazing rose, and lightly casting out, as it were, shining beams that give light. Also Isidore says that there is another kind which is very close to blue, and he is not all fiery but he has the virtue of heat, and there are five kinds of this, as Dioscorides says. Also Dioscorides says that the purple red is the most noble and better than the other, for the virtue of help against drunkenness, and it makes a man work, and puts away idle thoughts and makes good understanding; and it is soft, so that men can engrave in it and write. Kings clothe themselves in this colour when they hold court.

---

[90] Evans and Serjeantson read 're[d]yþ'.
[91] Evans and Serjeantson read 'f[i]ry'.

12

16. [Anancite]

Anittida is stone lik to oþer[92] stones þat begynnen by a; & his vertu is, if þu hast him þu maist commaund þe devell to þe, & he schal bere ouer þe se & þu wolt, & he schal do þe no harme.

Anancite is a stone similar to other stones that begin with A; and his virtue is that if you have him, you may command the devil to you, and he will obey you whatever you want to say, and he will do you no harm.

17. [Adredamia]

Adredamian lapis formi quasi tessera quadre / *Dicitur* argenti representare colorem / *Cuius* duricies quasi duricies adamantis / Ipse maris rubri mixtis reperitur arenis / Quam magus affirmat tantem virtutis haberi / Vt possit presens animos sedere volentes

Adredamia is a stone of a form like a four-sided tile; it is said to represent the colour of silver; its hardness is like the hardness of diamond. It is found in the Red Sea, mixed in with the sand; a magus affirms it has much of virtue, as, being present, it may be able to settle willing minds.

18. [Sapphire]

Aracontalides is a stone þat men clepeþ limecons brynge it in to ynd. It is purpill blak. If a man wasshe his mowþe & hold it vnnder his towngne, as longe as þe mone is waxing, a man may dyne[93] fro þe morne to midday, & þe cours to-for day, & wehen sche is prime þen her last her post al daye riȝt as when sche is of xv dayes full of age; his strengþe sholdith no lengere.

Sapphire is a stone that men called *limecons* bring into India. It is purple black. If a man washes his mouth and holds it under his tongue, as long as the moon is waxing, a man may divine from the morning until midday, and the course for the day, and when she is prime then her last her post all day just as when she is fifteen days old; his strength should hold no longer.

---

[92] Evans and Serjeantson have 'oper', which is a typographical error.
[93] Evans and Serjeantson read 'dy[uyn]'.

19. [Haematite]

Aricheces is a stone red shinyng as breññyng fire; & if þu wilt preve him, þrowȝt him into þe feyre & it schall wax pale. He þat bereþ þe stone & he be sike he schall neuer be hole.

Haematite is a shining red stone like burning fire; and if you want to prove him, throw him into the fire and it will grow pale. He who bears the stone, if he is sick, will never be whole.

20. [Akamanda]

<kadaman> Akamanda schineþ like water, & he is founde in þe water or reuer of nilus; and he is gode to a man þat bereþ him; þer schal no dedly wreþ ouercome him whilis he haþ it vpone him, so þat he lese not his vertue.

Akamanda shines like water, and he is found in the water of the river Nile; and he is good to a man who bears him; no deadly wrath will overcome him while he has it upon him, so that he does not lose his virtue.

21. [Cymophane]

Asterides & adiamante be wel ny lyke, for þey ben closed like togeder. Þis ston asterides is like a stare þer is no slne[94] so trobel þat schal cast clernes one him & þe firmament schal clere. All þe vertues he haþe as þes oþer þat begynneþ with a befor þis. Asterides is wyȝth & conteyneþ þe lyȝt þerynn I-closed, as it wer a ster goinge withyne, & maketh the sonne bemes lyȝt.

Cymophane and diamond are almost completely alike, for they are both enclosed together. This stone cymophane is like a star; there is no sun so cloudy that it will not cast clearness on him and the firmament will clear. He has all the virtues of these others that begin with 'A' before this. Cymophane is white and contains the light enclosed within it, and makes sunbeams light.

22. [Moonstone]

Astrion is a ston & it is lyk cristall, for he takeþ no colour, as schinyng lik þe sterres ben vp, for of þe sterres he takeþ his colour.

Moonstone is a stone and it is like crystal, for he takes no colour, as shining as are the stars above, for he takes his colour from the stars.

---

[94] Evans and Serjeantson read 's[o]ne'.

Also þer is anoþer stone of þe same colour þat mene clepen arechetes, & he schyneþ as brenyng feyr, as it is be-for seyd. Þis stone is founden in ynde, & in þe medel of þe stone þere is schynyng like a ster with clerenes of þe ful mone, & he haþ þe nam þat is clepid astris, **[fol. 3v]** for yf it is set in þe sterelyȝt it takeþ lyȝt of him, as Isodre seyþ, tᵒ de cristall.

Also there is another stone of the same colour that men call *arechetes*, and he shines like burning fire, as has been said before. This stone is found in India, and in the middle of the stone there is something shining like a star with the clearness of the full moon, and he has the name that is called *astris*, for if it is set in starlight it takes light from him, as Isidore says, in his book *Of Crystal*.

23. [Litharge of Silver]

Argirites is a ston lyk to syluer with golden spekkys.

Litharge of silver is a stone similar to silver with golden specks.

24. [Pyrite]

Andromia[95] is lyk þerto in colour, & it is a ston with þe colour of siluer; and Isodre seyþ it is iiij cornerd in schap as ben þe corners of a diamounde; & it is as stronge as þe ademant; & wyches seyen þat it haþe þat name for men wenen þat it refryneþ hastines & wraþe of hertes, as Isodr seyþ, sᵒ de gemmis.

Pyrite is similar to this in colour, and it is a stone with the colour of silver, and Isidore says it is four-cornered in shape as the corners of a diamond are, and it is as strong as the diamond; and witches say that it has that name because men suppose that it refines hastiness and wrath of hearts, as Isidore says in his summa *Of Gems*.

25. [Beryl]

Berellus

Berel is a stone & is browȝt owte of ynd, & it is myche worþe. Þis stone is lyk water & also myche

Beryl is a stone and is brought out of India, and it is of much value. This stone is like water and also

---

[95] Keiser (1992), p. 345 reads 'Andromaia'.

15

lyk cristall; & it haþe a rounde schap, some of gretnes of a napill & some lese. And whene þe sone schineþ, whiche comeþ owte of þe londe of ynde, þe rial berel casteþ feyr aȝens þe sone. The boke telliþ vs þat berell norschit loue betvxe man and woman; and wyȝt it well þe water where in it haþe leye his mych worþe to sor yene. And whoso drynk þe water þat it haþe leye in, it kepiþ him fro ȝexyng, & doþe away þe chafing of þe liuer; and whoso bereþ it schal be myche worchyped. The boke of dyuynyte seyþ to vs þat þe berell schal nat be scharp but pleyne & pulshid, when þe sone schynyth. The bible seyþ to vs þat owre lord god bad moyses to set berel þe xij stone in þe brest of arone. Sent Iohne seyþe in apocalyps þat þe berell is þe heyest in þe fundament. Also whose beriþ nyȝ to his flesche þe berel aȝens þe sone, þe feyr þat comeþ owte of ~~cha~~ catcheþ þe flesche; also þei þat taken þe berell & holden aȝens þe hote sone & holden lynen cloþ or flax or cotone, & þat schall wax one feyre þorowe of þe sone & þe vertu of þe stone. Ised seyþ þat þer bene x maners kynd of berel, & he haþe pale greynes, & þey schynne toward þe colour of gold; & þis ston cummeþ oute of ynde. Dias seyþe þe vertues of berell þat is most palle, þat berell is best aȝens stryfe, & makeþ þat a man may not be ouercum. Also he makeþ a man to be sufferable. Also he yeueþ gode witte, & he is

much like crystal; and it has a round shape, with some the same size as a nipple and some smaller. And when the sun shines, which comes out of the land of India, the real beryl casts fire against the sun. The book tells us that beryl nourishes love between man and woman; and understand well that the water in which it has lain is of much value to sore eyes. And whoever drinks the water that it has lain in, it keeps him from hiccoughing, and does away the chafing of the liver; and whoever bears it will be much honoured. The book of divinity says to us that the beryl should not be sharp but plain and polished when the sun shines. The Bible tells us that Our Lord God instructed Moses to set beryl as the twelfth stone in the breast of Aaron. St John says in the Apocalypse that the beryl is the highest in the foundation. Also whoever bears near to his flesh the beryl against the sun, the fire that comes out of it catches the flesh; also when people take the beryl and hold it against the hot sun and hold a linen cloth or flax or cotton, it will catch fire on account of the sun and the virtue of the stone. Isidore says that there are ten kinds of beryl, and they are pale grey, and they shine towards the colour of gold; and this stone comes out of India. Dioscorides describes the virtues of the beryl that is most pale; that beryl is best against strife, and ensures that a man may not be gode aȝens þe seknes of þe liuer, and also aȝens cherkyng & bolkyng; & he helpt most þen yne, & it brennit his hond þat bereþ it if it is holden before þe sone and makeþ a man g of grete astate & he loueþ well matremonye, and he holdeþ al þe sorrow of þe splene.

overcome. Also he allows a man to bear suffering. Also he gives good understanding, and he is good against the sickness of the liver, and also against retching and vomiting; and he helps most then in, and it burns the hand of him who holds it if it is held in front of the sun and makes a man of great estate, and he loves well matrimony, and he withholds all the sorrow of the spleen.

Berellus is a stone þat is wiȝt, somwhat grene; as it semeþ to þeyn yene-siȝt, a fowle of þe see is peyntyd withyn, & aboue a fase of best which [is] corniclam. If þu berest þis stone in a rynge, put a litel sauen vndire þe left kne, & þu schalt neuer be wroþ with þe woman þat þu hast weddid; also yf þu hast yuel in þin yne, grynd þis stone to powder, temper it with water, whas þeyn yen & þu schal be hole. Also it is seyd þat cristall is a maner kend of berell, & haþe pale greynes þer-of schinyng toward þe coleur of gold. Þat stone cumeth owt of ynde.

Beryl is a stone that is white, somewhat green, as it seems to your eyesight, a sea bird is painted inside it, and above it a face of a beast which is the unicorn. If you bear this stone in a ring, put a little savin juniper under the left knee, and you will never be angry with the woman you have wedded. Also if you have evil in your eyes, grind this stone to powder, temper it with water, wash your eyes and you will be whole. Also it is said that crystal is a type of beryl, and is of a pale grey colour shining towards the colour of gold. That stone comes out of India.

26. [Bericia]

Bericia is a ston, & he is like water. He is gode for swellyng in mennes belus; bet þat stone & grynd him to smal pouder, & drenk him, & he schal be hol of his swellyng of þe beleys.

Bericia is a stone that is like water. He is good for swelling in men's bellies; beat that stone and grind him to a fine powder and drink him, and he will be cured from his swelling of the belly.

27. [Belioculus]

[fol. 4r] Belloculyis is a stone, & he is like to berell. With-in him þer is a pirnell of clernes, & a-bowte him þer is a blak cirkel schynyng lyke ȝelowȝ gold. He þat bereþ þis stone schall neuer be dede in baytayle for no egge tole.

Belioculus is a stone that is similar to beryl. Within him there is a transparent spot, and around him there is a black circle shining like yellow gold. He who bears this stone will never die in battle from any edged tool.

28. [Badda]

Badda is a stone þat is well yuell to fynnd aboue all þe stones þat ben, for it schal neuer be founde but yf a man kerfe þe schip bordes, for it stekeþ so strongly þerin þat men may do it no harme, & no man may gete it with-owte keruyng of þe tre; & it haþe þe coler of rede, & semeþ all rede.

Badda is a stone that is extremely difficult to find, beyond all other stones there are, for it will never be found unless a man cuts into the ship boards, for it sticks so strongly on them that men may do it no harm, and no man may obtain it without cutting into a tree; and it has the colour of red, and seems all red.

29. [Bitumen]

Betumques is a stone of þe contrey of acherdes, & he is colour lyk to yerne; & he is of merwelows maners; & he is of þis kynde: if he be oones take & put to þe feyr, he schall bren all day & euer mor lastyng.

Bitumen is a stone of the country of Arcadia, and he is of a similar colour to iron; and he has marvellous properties; and he is of this kind: if he is once taken and put in the fire, he will burn all day and for evermore.

30. [Balas Ruby]

Baleis is a ston þat seynt Iohne cleped Iagounce; & it þrawit him to þe colour of rubie; & it is founde in a yel þat men clepen coracle, bytwene þe sees; & in þat yel so clepid is þis stone Iagounce founde, & it drawiþ to þe colour

The balas ruby is a stone that St John called jacinth, and it approaches the colour of ruby, and it is found in an island that men call Coracle, between the seas; and in that island, so called, jacinth is found, and it approaches of rubie, but he is not of þat maner, for when he is founde in places where men fynd him, þe rubies changen hem & amend his fayreness aȝens fayr tyme, & þe mor þey ben clere when þe tyme is cler. Þe Iagounce baleis is of mor gentil colour after þe rubie. Iagounce baleis; Iagounce saphir; Iagounce granet; cerryn; Iagounce þe gentil baleis. Owre lord ȝaue þer to many feyr vertues. The boke tellyþ vs þat whoso bereþ þe very many bayleis, & he schew it to his enemyis, he may turne aȝen hol & save; and whoso towcheþ þe iiij corners of his chambere or of his hall or of his gardyne, wormes ne tempest schal do no harme to þat howse. Also þat stone chayngeþ aȝens fayr tyme, & mendyþ her colour. Þe ston is found in an yle [*illeg.*] in the lond of Crope.

the colour of ruby, but he is not of that kind, for when he is found in the places where men find him, the rubies change him and amend his beauty against fair weather, and the clearer the weather the more transparent they are. The jacinth balas is of a more gentle colour than the ruby. Jacinth balas; jacinth sapphire; jacinth garnet; dried up jacinth; jacinth the gentle balas. Our Lord gave it many beautiful virtues. The book tells us that whoever bears very many balas rubies, and shows them to his enemies, he may return again whole and safe; and whoever touches the four corners of his chamber or of his hall or of his garden, neither worms nor tempest will do harm to that house. Also that stone changes against fair weather, and amends her colour. The stone is found in an island in the land of Crope.

31. [Chrysolite]

Crisolide recembleþ mich to þe water of þe see, & castyþ a flawme a[96] it wer of gold by euery syde. Þe boke seyþ þat it were gode to bere amoung kyndly stones; and who-so be owte of dedly synne & of schrewdnes, he may enter into many cowrtes & contreys with eny aȝenseyng; and all men schall bere grace to him. And as þe bokes tellen vs þat who-so haþe crisolide persed &

Chrysolite greatly resembles seawater, and casts a beam like gold on every side. The book says that it is good to bear among kindly stones; and whoever is not in mortal sin and is of good judgement may enter into many courts and countries without any gainsaying; and all men will bear grace to him. And the books tell us that whoever has a pierced chrysolite put through a bristle

---

[96] Evans and Serjeantson read 'a[s]'.

put þorow a brestell here of an asse he schall mow go a-monge develles, & hafe hem by nyȝt with-owt eny dowt; and as bokes seyþ þat who-so beryþ þis stone he schall [kepe] his body trewly. It schall be bore on þe lefte syde. Crisolide comeþ owte of ethiopie. Also crisolide bereþ colour of þe see water & of gold. Sent Iohne seyþe in þe apocolyps þat he sey crisolide þe vj ston in þe fundament of þe wery kyngdome. The bible seyþ þat crysolide was in the brest of aarone. Also Ised seyþe þat þer is anoþer maner of crisolide þat is clepid crisoletus, & he is colerd as gold; & he is well fayer in syȝt in þe moruntyde, & þen as þe daye passeþ his coler waxeþ dyme. Þis stone takeþ most soone & if to be set by þe feyr anone it waxeþ into a lyȝe.

hair of a donkey will go more among devils, and have them by night without any doubt. And the books say that whoever bears this stone will keep his body truly. It should be borne on the left side. Chrysolite comes out of Ethiopia. Also chrysolite bears the colour of seawater and of gold. St John says in the Apocalypse that chrysolite is the sixth stone in the foundation of the very kingdom. The Bible says that chrysolite was in the breast of Aaron. Also Isidore says that there is another kind of chrysolite that is called chrysolete, and he is the colour of gold; and he is very beautiful to the sight in the morning, and then as the day passes his colour becomes dim. This stone takes most sun, and if it is set by the fire it soon grows into a light.

32. [Chalcedony]

Calcidonice is a ston of white pale coler, as it were a trobel whitnes; & it comeþ owt of þe est, & it is lik to cristal; & he þat bereþ [fol. 4v] him schall [be] well spekyng & ful of gret eloquens; & if he [haue] eny ple or cause, schwe þe stone to his aduersary, & it schall helpe him in his cause, & if he pleded with wrounge it helpit him in his riȝt. He þat bereþ þe sardyne, þe onycle & calsidonye, he schall be well entacched, but yf he lese his vertu þorowȝ synne. The calsedony bereþ grace to him

Chalcedony is a stone of white pale colour, as it were a cloudy whiteness; and it comes out of the east, and it is similar to crystal; and he who bears him will be well spoken and of great eloquence; and if he has any plea or cause, let him show the stone to his adversary, and it will help him in his cause; and if he pleaded against wrong it will help him in his right. He who bears sardine, onyx and chalcedony will be well enriched, unless he loses his virtue through sin. Chalcedony bears þat bereþ hi*m*; and if a ma*n* be iuged þorow fals iugeme*nt* þ*is* wol nat leue fro hi*m* þat he schall not be lost fro*m* hi*m*; & he schall loue þe seruice of god whiles he bereþ hi*m* clen. Also Isod seyþe þat þe ston is ge*n*dryd of reyn*e* of yow*er* lord*es* as it is seyd; and he is fou*n*de i*n* þe full of þe mone; & he is not fou*n*de but of iij colo*urs*, as þe lapidare seyþ þ*at* all ky*n*de þ*er*of w*ith*-þraweþ grauy*n*ge, & drawyþ to hi*m*-self strawe if he be het or chafyd. Ised seyþe if þ*is* ston be p*er*sed & Ibore makeþ a ma*n* to haue maystre i*n* causes, and it help*it* a3e*n* iapis & scornes of fee*n*des, & kepeþ & saueth v*er*tues as diascorides seyþ*e*.

grace to him who bears him, and if a man is judged through false judgement this will not be lost from him; and he will love the service of God while he bears him in purity. Also Isidore says that the stone is born of rain of your lords, as it is said; and he is found at the full moon; and he is only found in three colours, since the lapidary says that all kinds of chalcedony withstand engraving, and he draws to himself straw if he is struck or rubbed. Isidore says that if this stone is pierced and borne it gives a man mastery in causes, and it helps against tricks and scorns of fiends, and keeps and saves virtues, as Dioscorides says.

33. [Chrysoprase]

Crisopas is a ston*e* & it is brou3t oute of þe lond of ynde. Þe bokes tellyn*e* vs þ*at* his colo*ur* is gren, & þey ben lyk hogg*es* yen, & þey caste oute as gold by al sydes. Who-so bereþ it, me*n* schal be glad & ioyfull of his co*m*myng. This crisopas comeþ owte of ynd þe more. And som me*n* seye*n* his colo*ur* is lyk þe Iues of apples, & he schew*it* lyke to gold; and [he] þ*at* bereþ hi*m* schall be ful of gr*a*ce, & be loued of all me*n* & wome*n*. And some me*n* seyne þat þ*is* ston comeþ oute of ~~Egype~~ ethiope; & he schyneþ moche in þe ny3t.

Chrysoprase is a stone that is brought out of the land of India. The books tell us that his colour is green, and they are like pigs' eyes, and they cast out gold beams on all sides. Whoever bears it, men will be glad and joyful at his coming. This chrysoprase comes out of the greater India. And some men say his colour is like the apple juice, and he appears like gold; and he who bears him will be full of grace, and will be loved of all men and women. And some men say that this stone comes out of Ethiopia, and he shines much in the night.

34. [Chilindris]

Chilindris lap*is* volubil[is] *in* modu*m* colu*mp*ne quaidra coegit.

The stone chilindris forms itself in the manner of a winding column of four sides.

35. [Coramis]

Coramis albus et durus.

Coramis is white and hard.

36. [Cinaedia]

Cemedia lapis q*uis* i*n*ue*nitur in* cerebr*o* pisc*is* eiusde*m* no*m*i*n*is.

Cinaedia is a stone which is found in the brain of a fish of the same name.

37. [Cameo]

Cemieus lapis fla*mm*e*us* a color*e* dittus.

Cameo is a rich stone of fiery red colour.

38. [Calluca]

Calluca e*st* gemma viridis color*is*.

Calluca is a gem of green colour.

39. [Crystal]

Cristallus is a stone þ*at* co*n*ceyueþ wel fyr*e* of þe son*e* bem. Also make poud*er* þ*er*-of, gif it to þe nurse to þry*n*ke, & it schal i*n*crese her mylke & multiplye it anon*e*. Also c*r*istall haþ þ*at* v*er*tue, þ*at* if eny ston*e* haþ*e* lost his v*er*tu þorow3 synne, let hi*m* co*n*fes hi*m* of his sy*n*ne, & take & wasche þe c*r*istall i*n* feyr wat*er* & towche þe ston þerewyþ, & ano*n* he schall tak his v*er*tu a3en by þe v*er*tu of c*r*istall. Some me*n* sey*n* þ*at* he is harded by gret cold, & so he becomeþ c*r*istall. Also he kepeþ a

Crystal is a stone that makes fire well from sunlight. Also make powder from it, give it to the nurse to drink, and it will increase her milk and soon multiply it. Also crystal has this virtue, that if any stone has lost his virtue through sin, let a man confess his sin, and take and wash the crystal in pure water and touch the stone with it, and soon he will take his virtue again by the virtue of the crystal. Some men say he is made hard by great cold, and so he becomes crystal. Also he keeps a man chast, & makeþ a man myche worchipid; and men seyne þat it come owte of ynde & of araby; and old anceters tellin þat it is harden by froste; & some men contrarien þe old maisters; and so many contraries þer bene þat it is not of so gret coldnes. Also Ised seyþe cristall is a briȝt stone & colerd with watery coler. Manye trowen þat snowe or yesse is mad hard in spas of many yers, & þer-for þe grekes ȝafe a name þer-to, þat it is gendred in aseie & in cipres & namely in þe norþe mowntens þer þe sonne is most feruent in somer, & þerfor þey maken yesse to dure loung, & þat þey clepen cristall. Þis stone, Iset anone in þe sone, it takeþ feyre & lyȝt þat he setteþ drie taddestoles afeyr. His vse is ordeyned to drynk and worchep, no oder þinge but what cold þyng may suffre. Also dias seyþ of cristal, & seyþe þat it is hard and torned into a ston, not only by vertu of strengþe of cold but mor by erdly vertu. Þe colour þer of [fol. 5r] is lyk to yesse. Also þrenk it & it helpit aȝens colica passio.

Hunc et tritum quidam cum melle propinant partibus infantes quibus assygnantur alendi / Quo potu credunt repleti vbera latte.

man chaste, and makes a man much honoured; and men say that it comes out of India and Arabia; and old ancestors tell that it is hardened by frost; and some men contradict the old masters, and so there are many contrary opinions that it is not of great coldness. Also Isidore says that crystal is a bright stone and coloured with watery colour. Many assert that snow or ice is made hard in the space of many years, and therefore the Greeks gave it a name, that it is born in Asia and in Cyprus and namely in the north mountains where the sun is strongest in summer, and therefore they make ice last long. This stone, set for a short while in the sun, makes fire and light that sets dry toadstools alight. His use is ordained to drink and honour, nothing else but what a cold thing may allow. Also Dioscorides speaks of crystal, and says that it is hard and turned into a stone not only by the virtue or strength of cold but rather by earthly virtue. Its colour is similar to ice. Also drink it and it helps against colic.

And there is a certain custom when they offer drink with honey, by which parts infants are given nourishment; by this drink they believe breasts are filled with milk.

40. [Celidony]

Celidonie is a stone þat men fynd in þe wombe of a swallow. Sche is not feyr, but not for þen sche is moche valowur & mor þen eny oþer stones in profyte. Of þes stones þer ben too maneres; þer bene þe one blake & þat oþer red; þe red is gode aȝens a malady þat men clepen lunatix, wherby he falleþ, & wherby he is foolych & wytles & falleþ þer-with long tyme; let him ber þis ston & it will make him well to spek & wel to be loued and syde. But þe blak stone, & a man bere it in such maner, it schal help to do grete þynges. It helpeþ aȝens malices of gret princes & kynges. Þe water þat It Is wasshen in is myche worþe to hot yueles. Also it is miche worþ þis stone, if it be hold at þe sacrament & be wounden in linen cloþe, withholdeþ þe feuer & aȝen stondeþ wycked humours þat comen abowte in many maners; and if it be wasshen & if ben in clen water it is gode for sor yene.

Celidony is a stone which men find in the womb of a swallow. She is not beautiful, but nevertheless she is of much value and more profitable than any other stone. There are two kinds of these stones; there is one black and another red. The red is good against a malady which men call lunacy, in which a man stumbles, and in which he is foolish and without judgement and suffers from this for a long time. Let him bear this stone and it will make him speak well and to be well loved. But if a man bears the black stone in this way, it will help him to do great things. It helps against malice of great princes and kings. The water it is washed in is of much value to hot evils. Also this stone is very valuable if it is held up at the sacrament and is wound in a linen cloth; it withholds the fever and withstands wicked humours that come about in many ways, and if it is washed in pure water it is good for sore eyes.

41. [Coral]

Coral is a ston þat groweþ in þe red see as an erbe þat is gren, & when it is owte in þe eyr it wexyþ hard & red & recembleth to a branche, & it is no more þen half a fote, & it is mych louely to him þat bereþ it. And þe old autors seyn, ȝerastros, Methodorus, & þe

Coral is a stone that grows in the Red Sea as a plant that is green, and when it is out in the air it becomes hard and looks like a branch, and it is no more than half a foot, and it is very lovely to him who bears it. And the old authors say – Zoroaster, Methodorus, and gode auto*ur* phytonas, it þedfendeþ te*m*pest i*n* þe plas þer it is, and þe stone is gode to set i*n* a vyn*n*ȝerd, or i*n* gardynes or feldis, for it kepeþ away te*m*pest & all yuel, & makeþ þe fruyte to multiply. And he delyueriþ a ma*n* fro fa*n*taseys; an*e* it yeveþ a gode begy*n*nyng & a gode ending, & stancheþ blod and he is gode for þe fowle yuel. Þis corall is lyke raue flesch ywash, redische. Also whoso bereþ þis stone vpon*e* hi*m* or on*e* his fynger, he schal get loue; and if he haue ey[97] siknes vpon*e* hi*m* he schal son*e* be hol. Also powder of þis stone ydro*n*ke is riȝt good for þe crampe. Also ysodre seyþe i*n* cci° de ge*m*mis rubeis þat it foloweþ þer þat as p*r*ecyus ston*n*es þat margarite is amo*n*ge vs, so p*r*eciose or more is þe coral amo*n*ge þe yendes. Wycches telle*n* þat þis stone wiþsto*n*diþ lyȝtynge; and Ised sayþ þe same, þat it putteth away te*m*pest & whirlewy*n*des. All aucto*ur*s sey*n* þat corall is corall is gode & help*in*g agay*n* þe fowle yuel, for þe fendes gile, for schorny*n*g, for to stau*n*che blode, for wou*n*des, for þe crampe, for gardyns, for to multepley fruyte, for make god begy*n*nyng, for to make gode endy*n*ng of causes & redes. Also þer is wyȝt corall, & it haþe all þe ve*r*tues þat þe rede corall haþe & moo. If a ma*n* have sore yen, or sore teeþ, or sor i*n* þe rofe of þe mowþe þat be full of

the good author Phytonas – that it defends against tempest in the place where it is, and the stone is good to set in a vineyard, or in gardens or fields, for it keeps away tempests and all evil, and makes fruit multiply. And he delivers a man from fantasies, and it gives a good beginning and a good ending, and staunches blood, and he is good for the foul evil. This coral is like raw flesh when washed, reddish. Also whoever bears this stone upon him or on his finger, he will obtain love; and if he has any sickness upon him he will soon be whole. Also powder of this stone drunk is very good for the cramp. Also Isidore says in his two hundred and first chapter about red gems that it follows there that as the pearl is a precious stone among us, so is the coral among the Indians. Witches say that this stone withstands light-ning; and Isidore says the same, that it puts away tempests and whirlwinds. All authors say that coral is good and helpful against the foul evil, for the fiend's guile, for ridicule, for staunching blood, for wounds, for the cramp, for gardens, to multiply fruit, to make a good beginning, to make a good ending of causes and counsels. Also there is white coral, and it has all the virtues that the red coral has and more. If a man has sore eyes, or sore teeth, or sore in the roof of

---

[97] Evans and Serjeantson read 'e[n]y'.

25

bleders, take þe wyȝt corall & g[r]inde him small, & temper it with water, & wissh þin yene þerwith & þey mowthe & they teeþ, & þeyn bleders schall be holl. Also yf a man or a woman haue þe blody mensyone, þrynk þe powder of þis ston, & þey schal be hole & if þu wilt bere þis ston þu most perse him & þen bere þat stone. All þe vertues he haþ as all þe stones that begenyne with [fol. 5v] C C C.

the mouth that is full of blisters, take the white coral and grind him to small pieces, and mix it with water, and wash your eyes with it and your mouth and your teeth, and your blisters will be whole. Also if a man or woman has the bloody flux, drink the powder of this stone, and they will be whole; and if you want to bear this stone you must pierce him and then bear that stone. He has all the virtues of all the stones that begin with C.

42. [Cinaedia]

Cymydia is a stone, & he is founnd in þe hedd of a fisch; & is longe stone & a wiȝt. If a man bereþ him in his mowþe þer schall no tempest in water du him harme neder by lond, ne he schall neuer be scomfited in were.

Cinaedia is a stone that is found in the head of a fish; and it is a long stone and white. If a man bears him in his mouth no tempest on water will do him harm, nor on land, nor will he ever be discomforted in war.

43. [Cimbria]

Cymbria is a ston þat comeþ of a fissh of þe see, & þat fyssh men clepen ȝele⁹⁸; þis ston is wyȝt & dry as chalk. He þat bereþ þis stone schall be mery & laxatyf, & he schal neuer be gret scleper, ne he schal neuer tak gret colde in water ne in londe.

Cimbria is a stone that comes from a fish in the sea, and that fish men call eel; this stone is white and as dry as chalk. He who bears this stone will be merry and relaxed, and he will never be a great sleeper, nor will he ever suffer from great cold on water or on land.

---

[98] Evans and Serjeantson read 'ȝele' as a scribal mistranscription of 'cete', meaning a whale.

44. [Collorus]

Collorus is a stone, & is lyke a sapher but he [is] wyȝte in schynyng as water of the see. He þat bereþ þis ston percede abowte his nyke schal neuer dedly wraþe of euencristene; & he schall haue a man fro wyckyd spirites; þat he deseyreþ riȝtfully he schal haue.

Collorus is a stone which is similar to a sapphire, but he is white in shining like seawater. He who bears this stone pierced around his neck will never incur the deadly wrath of any Christian; and he will protect a man from wicked spirits; he will have what he rightfully desires.

45. [Capnite]

Capnices is a stone lyke cristall; þu schalt not knowe þat one fro þat oder, safe þis capnice is wyȝtter þen þe cristall. He þat bereþ þis ston schal not haue þe dropsy, & it schall defen him fro wyckyd enchauntementes; & if a man be seke & drynk of þis ston he schal neuer be hole; þis preued euax þe kynge.

Capnite is a stone similar to crystal; you will not know the one from the other, except that capnite is whiter than the crystal. He who bears this stone will not have the dropsy, and it will defend him from wicked enchantments; and if a man is sick and drinks from this stone he will never be whole; Evax the king proved this.

46. [Corinth]

Corinthe is a ston blac & rounde, & it is myche worþe aȝens venymynge of bestes, as of adders & oþer. If a man stamp it with oyle roset, & bereþ it amounge \With hym/ wylde best when he goþe in desert, & haue with corenthe, he dar not reche of hurtyng of edders. Þe þrid maner is more preysed, for it is one party scharp & one þat oþer partie as it were yern grounde. A woman þat bereþ it one here, it causeþ perel to þe chil in here wombe.

Corinth is a black and round stone, and it is of very great value against poisoning by beasts, such as by adders and others. If a man stamps it with oil of roses and bears it among wild beasts when he travels in deserted places, and has corinth with him, he need not fear injury from adders. The third kind is more prized, for it it is partly sharp and partly as if ground by iron. If a woman bears it on her it causes peril to the child in her womb.

47. [Toadstone]

Crapadoune, ne serpentes townge, ne many of oþer stones to þe wych god haþ ȝeuen vertu be not ynoumbred amonge þe xxxvj stones befor nemed, for carpadone is founde in þe hede of carpadonie þat is of vii ȝere old & mor; & sche þat bereþ þis ston, wene sche meteþ with a man comyng aȝens here, sche ryseþ vpone her fete behynd with gret stregþe by þe vertu of þis stone. And þis stone is half broune & half wyȝt al abowte. And he þat will haue þis stone, he most he most take þe crepaud & put him in a new pote of erþe, & make þer-in many holys, & set it in an Ant-hell, & keuer þe pott aboue; And þen schall þe antes ete þe crepaude all save þe bones, and þu schalt fynde þe stone styk one þe hed of þe crepaude. And he is god for venym, & he most be set in fyne gold; and some seyne, þat it is blak and is gode for medecyne & for venym, and þer as he is may no yuel be done. And he makeþ a man & woman myȝty; also he makeþ a man to incres fro day to day, & abounde in worthinnes. And some seyne þat þer is one of þe colour of wax, & he is gode to conquer batayls.

Toadstone, or serpent's tongue, or many other stones to which God has given virtues are not enumerated among the thirty-six stones before named, for toadstone is found in the head of a toad which is seven years old or more; and she who bears this stone, when she meets with a man coming against her, rises on her hind feet with great strength, by the virtue of this stone. And this stone is half brown and half white all over. And whoever wants to have this stone must take the toad and put him in a new earthenware pot, and make many holes in it, and put it in an ant hill, and cover over the pot; and then the ants will eat all of the toad except the bones, and you will find the stone stuck on the head of the toad. And he is good for venom, and he must be set in fine gold; and some say it is black and good for medicine and for venom, and wherever he is no evil may be done. And he makes a man or woman mighty; and he makes a man increase from day to day, and abound in worthiness. And some say that there is one of the colour of wax, and he is good to win battles.

48. [Calciphane]

Caltophono is a stone þat is blake, & it makeþ a man to haue a swete & cleyr voys. If a man bere þis

Calciphane is a stone that is black, and it gives a man a sweet and clear voice. If a man bears this ston vpone him, he most be mek þat schall bere him.

stone on him, he must be meek who wants to bear him.

49. [Calastida]

Caladista is a ston þat haþe þe colour lyk sendres. Þe woman þat þrenkeþ it with oyle, it schall multepley her mylke; but sche most vse it befor met or after badyng; and if it be perced & an her of wole of a schep þat is with lambe & be put þorow, & hanked at þe norseis neke, it scha mych awayl her; and if a woman trauell with child, let her bynd it to her þeyȝe. And if a woman make povder þer of & temper it with salt & water, & noynte here within & withowte, it schal awayll [fol. 6r] myche. And þe water avayleþ myche þe schorpe[99] fro þe reme. Also þe old autors seyn it schall as myche avayle as all.

Calastida is a stone that has a colour like ash. If a woman drinks it with oil it will multiply her milk; but she must use it before meat or after bathing. And if it is pierced and a hair of wool of a sheep that is with lamb is put through, and hung at the nurse's neck, it will be a great help to her; and if a woman labours with child, let her bind it to her thigh. And if a woman makes powder from it and tempers it with salt and water, and anoints herself inside and out, it will be a great help. And the water greatly helps the sheep from the rheum. Also the old authors say it is as much a help as anything.

50. [Carnelian]

Corneole is a derke stone, & not-for-þan it haþe gret vertu. It fordoþe wraþ, & it haþe colour like blake flessh, and it well stanche blod of all membres, & namly wemmen þat han ouer-myche her flowres.

Carnelian is a dark stone, but nonetheless it has great virtue. It prevents wrath, and it has a colour like black flesh, and it will staunch blood from all limbs, and especially women who suffer from excessive periods.

51. [Calonite]

Calonite is a stone þat is called fre, & he is lyk to purpill color, & he is founde in ynde. If a man put

Calonite is a stone that is called free, and he is close to a purple colour, and he is found in India. If

---

[99] Evans and Serjeantson read 'sch[e]pe'.

hi*m* in his mowþe erly in þe moru*n*tide til þe owr of sixe i*n* þe waxi*n*ge of þe mone, he may deuyne al þ*at* is aft*er* to come, & e*n*creseþ & decreseþ as þoþe þe mone; and whene þe mone is pryme, þ*en* duret his my3t al day. Þis stone wil not bren w*ith* eny man*er* feyr. And some seyne it draweþ Iaspyne colo*ur*. And he is mich worþ to ladies, for he norsheþ loue & w*ith*-holdeþ loue. And he is god for the tisik.

And som*e* seyn*e* it comeþ owte of persce.

a man puts him in his mouth early in the morning until the sixth hour of the waxing of the moon, he may divine all that is to come after, and increases and decreases as does the moon; and when the moon is prime, then his power lasts all day. This stone will not burn with any kind of fire. And some say it approaches the colour of jasper. And he is of very great value to ladies, for he nourishes love and withholds love. And he is good for the tisic.

And some say it comes out of Persia.

52. [Thegolite]

Cecolite is a stone þ*at* is fowle to be-hold on*e*, but he is of a p*r*ecius nature. Þe ston leyd i*n* wat*er* & ydrou*n*k a gode draw3t þ*er*-ofe, is god for þe reynes, and he is gode to clense þe entrayles w*ith*yne forþe.

Thegolite is a stone that is ugly to look at, but he is of a precious nature. If the stone is laid in water and drunk with a good draught of it, it is good for the kidneys, and he is good to purify the entrails within.

53. [Thunderstone]

Ceramus is a stone þ*at* comeþ of araby, and who þ*at* bereþ it, þ*is* stone, vpone hi*m*, it wole bere hi*m* fro weders & horrible te*m*pest & yuel eyr*is*, as ly3tnyn*g* of fyr & þonder. And some sey*n* þ*at* it comeþ owte of grek; & he wol be se bor mekely; and it haþe his name of a flume i*n* grek þ*at* þ*is* stone is fou*n*de in; and þis ston is god for flodes. And he þ*at* bereþ hi*m* schal not be dre*n*ched i*n* eny

Thunderstone is a stone that comes from Arabia, and whoever bears this stone upon him it will protect him from weather and horrible tempests and evil airs, such as lightning of fire and thunder. And some say that it comes out of Greece; and he should be borne meekly; and it takes its name from a river in Greece that this stone is found in; and this stone is good for floods.

flod; ne þer schall no howse, ne towne, ne marener in þe se be anoyed with flod þer þis ston is. And he is gode fore bateles & victories. And he ʒeueþ swet slepes & swete dremes to a man. And some seyne þat he [is] lyke to cristall & coral for he is of suche dowble colowre. Also ysidr & Lapidary seyn, when it þondreþ horribly, þe feyr of þe eyr leyʒtneþ, whene c[l]owdes smyten togeder þis ston falleþ fro heuen.

And he that bears him will not be drenched in any flood; nor shall any house, or town, or mariner in the sea be annoyed with flood where this stone is. And he is good for battles and victories. And he gives sweet sleeps and sweet dreams to a man. And some say that he is similar to crystal and coral for he is of such double colour. Also Isidore and the lapidary say that when it thunders horribly, the fire of the air produces lightning, and when clouds strike together this stone falls from heaven.

54. [Cataricus]

Cataricus is a stone, & is fownden in þe see, & þer it is norsched. Þe ston is gode for leche-crafte, as for ycche in þe body, for þe scabe, for serpige, & impetige. Make powder þer-of, & ley it in veneger al a nyʒt; & þen take þe powder of lyterg, of gold, & oyle of roses, & make her-of an oynente & noynte þe sores þerwith.

Cataricus is a stone that is found in the sea, and there it is nourished. The stone is good for leechcraft, such as for an itch in the body, for scabies, eczema and impetigo. Make powder from it and lay it in vinegar all night; and then take the powder of litharge, of gold, and oil of roses, and make an ointment from them and anoint the sores with it.

55. [Thunderstone]

Coparius is a stone þat is bred in þe eyre, & some callen it fouldre; & he falleþ with a tempest to þe erþe when gret tempest of þondres & lyʒtnyng fallen, & it falleþ in to þe erþe ix fote, & þe erþe reboundeþ aʒene agayne be vertu of þe ston. And he þat <c> secþ after him schall not fynd him til ix

Thunderstone is a stone which is bred in the air, and some call it 'fouldre', and he falls with a tempest to the earth when great tempests of thunder and lightning happen, and it falls into the earth nine feet, and the earth rebounds against it again by virtue of the stone. And he that seeks after him dayes be passed. Þe man þat most ber þis ston most kepe him clen fro lechery, & þen schall no tempest do him harme in lond ne in vater ne no mysauentur[100] do him harme ne come to him.

will not find him until nine days have passed. The man who must bear this stone must keep himself pure from lechery, and then no tempest will do him harm, neither on land nor on water will any misadventure do him harm nor come to him.

56. [Celidony]

Cleridonius is a ston, & þer ben two of hem; þat one is blak, þat oþer is red; & boþe þey ben rounde in ligging. He þat bereþ þis in his left harme he schal not be sclaw; & he schal be a feyr speker, & he schal be loued of all men; and he þat bereþ þis blak stone, what þyng he begenneþ ryȝtfully he scha mak a gode ende. And yf a mannes [fol. 6v] yene dropene sore, make powdere of þis ston, & wash þyne yene þerwith, & þey schal be hole. Also for a codidiane feuer & a tercian feuer, bynde þis stone in a red sendell clowte, & ber it vpone þe, & þu schalt be hole. Also yf a woman be in trauelyng of a child, by þe vertu of þis ston sche schall be delyuerd with gret peyne of her body, & þe chyld þis stone may touche ne dieþ.

Celidony is a stone of which there are two kinds: one is black, the other is red; and they are both round in shape. Whoever bears this on his left arm will not be slain; and he will be a fair speaker, and he will be loved of all men; and whoever bears this black stone, whatever he begins rightfully he will make a good end of. And if a man's eyes are very downcast, make powder of this stone, and wash your eyes with it, and they will be whole. Also for a quotidian fever and a tertian fever, bind this stone in a red sindon cloth, and bear it upon you, and you will be whole. Also if a woman is labouring with child, by the virtue of this stone she will be delivered with great pain of her body, and the child this stone touches will not die.

57. [Carbuncle]

Carbuncculus is a precios stone, & he schineþ as feyre whose schynyng is not ouercom by nyȝt.

Carbuncle is a precious stone, and he shines like fire whose shining is not overcome by night. It shines

---

[100] Evans and Serjeantson have 'mysaueutur', a typographical error.

32

It schineþ in derk places, & it semeþ as it were a feyr; & þer bene xij kyndes þer-of, & worþyest ben þo þat schynen & send owte leemes as feyre, as Ised. Also it is seyd þat þe carbunocyl is cleped so in grek, & it is gendryd in libia amonge þe tregodites. Of þis carbuncul þer is xij maneris of kendes of carbuncles. But þoo ben best þat han þe coleour of fire & þo ben closed in a wyȝt veyne. The best carbucul haþe þis propirtie: if it is ꝺ þrowene In þe feyre it is qwent as it were amonges dede colis, & it is brennyt yf water be þorow þer-of. Anoder kynde of carbuccle is cleped starida sirus, & he haþe þat name of a plase of ynde in whiche he is founde In þis maner of kynd, as it were withyn hit bryȝt feyre ben ysey, as it were droppis of gold. And þes precious stones ben of gret price withoute comparison þen ben þe oder. And þer is anoþer maner kynd þat haþe signes, & he haþe þe name of smellynge of lanternys, & þis preciowus stone is clepid remissus carbuncels, not þat it is chef carbuncclus; and here of dowbel maner of kynd, þat oone is with bemes of purpull colour of red sylk; and þis kynd if it be hotte in þe sone with fretyng of fynggers, it wol þraue to himself <r> straues & leevys of bokys. Also it is seyd þat it withstondet grauyng, & it is some tyme ygraue & Iprentyd in wex as it were with byȝtyng of a best, as Ised seyþ. Amonge þe

in dark places, and it seems like a fire, and there are twelve kinds of it, and the most valuable is that which shines and sends out beams like fire, as Isidore says. Also it is said that the carbuncle is so called in Greek, and it is produced in Libya among the troglodytes. Of this carbuncle there are twelve kinds. But the best ones are those that have the colour of fire and they are enclosed in a white vein. The best carbuncle has this property: if it is thrown into the fire it is marvellous, as if it were among dead coals, and it is burnt if water is thrown on it. Another kind of carbuncle is called *starida sirus*, and he has that name from a place in India where he is found in this way, as it were seen within a bright fire, like spots of gold. And these precious stones are of great price without comparison with anything else. And there is another kind that has signs, and he has the name 'smelling of lanterns', and these precious stones are called watery carbuncles, because they are not the greatest carbuncles. And there are two kinds of these, one with beams of purple colour of red silk; and this kind, if it is heated in the sun with rubbing of fingers, will draw to himself straws and leaves of books. Also it is said that it withstands engraving, and it is sometimes engraved and printed in wax as if with the biting of a beast, as Isidore says. Among the kinds of carbuncles is counted the maner of kynd, of carbu*nccus*, belagius is acou*nt*ed, þ*at* is red & briʒt, as dia seyþ. Also it is seyd þ*at* þ*is* man*er* of carbu*n*ccle is þe vayn*e* of saphir*e*. Belagius haþ*e* a man*er* myʒt as it wer aboute sp*er*kynge of fyr*e* þ*at* beclyppeþ hi*m* w*it*howte, and þ*is* is ope*n*ly Iseyn yf me*n* tak besily hede þ*er*-to.

balas ruby, which is red and bright, as Dioscorides says. Also it is said that this kind of carbuncle is the vein of sapphire. The balas ruby has a kind of power to spark fire that strikes him outside, and this is plainly seen if men pay careful attention to it.

58. [Chrysopase]

Crisopass*us* is a ston of ethiopie, & it is hide in lyʒt & seen*e in* derkeness, for it is firy by niʒt & goldy by day, as Isodr*e* seyþe; þ*er*fore he is hid be day, as it were wesshynge, & waxeþ pal as gold. & anoþ*er* man*er* kynd þ*at* is clepid crispass*us* ıs lıke *in* colo*ur* to a ston þ*at* is called prassius, & it [is] grene as lyk, as it is besprenge w*ith* certeyn*e* dropis of gold, as it is seyde in þe lapidary of bartholomewe.

Chrysopase is a stone of Ethiopia, and it is hidden in light and seen in darkness, for it is fiery by night and golden by day, as Isidore says; therefore he is hidden by day, as if made of gold, and grows as pale as gold. And another kind which is called chrysopase ıs similar in colour to a stone that is called prase, and it is just as green, as it is mottled with certain spots of gold, as it is said in the lapidary of Bartholomaeus Anglicus.

59. [Diamond]

Diamand is a ston þ*at* is named & dyuysed *in* þe lapidary, for euax, ky*ng* of araby, seyþ to vs þ*at* diamand þ*at* comeþ owte of ynd ben clepid þe mal, & þey ben brewe*n* of colo*ur* & of violet, & þo þ*at* come*n* owte of araby be*n* clepid þe femal, & þey ben more whiʒt, resonable to þe colo*ur* of c*r*istall. A diamand is no mor þen a lytel note, but he is mor hard of all stones. No ma*n* may amend

Diamond is a stone that is named and described in the lapidary, for Evax king of Arabia tells us that the diamond which comes out of India is called the male, and they are brown and violet in colour; and those which come out of Arabia are called female, and they are more white, similar to the colour of crystal. A diamond is no more than a little nut, but he is harder than all stones. No man can him of bewte ne polissh him, ne for no noþþyng. Of such man*er* þey ben foun*de* and **[fol. 7r]** bore *in* gold. Þe lapidar*e* seyþ vs þ*at* god ȝaue ma*ny* fayr*e* ve*r*tues & *gra*ce to þe diamond, þ*at* if a man ber*e* it in stren*þ* & v*er*tu, it kepi*t* him fro greuance, meti*nges* & temtacions, & fro venym. Also it kep*it* þe bones i*n* þe me*m*bres hole, so-fer*e*-forþ þ*at* þu schalt not fale of horse ne of oþ*er* best but þ*at* þe bone schal be-leue hole, who þ*at* bereþ it i*n* clen leuy*ng*. Also it defendiþ þe þred that comeþ be nyȝt; & it doþe away heuy wrath & lechery; and it kepeþ a ma*n* in þe same poy*nt* þ*at* he fyndeþ him, of prys, of wytte, of walew, of riches, & encresyþ him in valew, i*n* riches & good, ne he schal not be made lese; & he schall be of lytel dispense if he clenly ber it. A diamau*nd* is myche worthe to be-hold on*e* for wytles me*n*; and it defendeþ him fro his enemyis; & þ*at* bereþ, he schal þe mor loue god; also it kepeþ þe sed of ma*n* wyþi*n*ne þe wombe of his wyfe, & it helpeþ þe child & kepeþ þe childis me*m*bres hole. Þe bokes seyne vs þ*at* if a woma*n* be w*ith* child it most be borne on*e* þe lefte seyd. And whoso wil p*r*eue [h]is ve*r*tu he most haue it of trew bey*i*ng, or*e* of ȝifte, & hole & holy schal he be þ*at* þis ston bereþ in clen*n*es; & it is most Iborne on þe lifte syde of a ma*n* or*e* of a woma*n*; & þen he haþe ve*r*tu. Also þis stone is not made w*ith* yerne ne stell ne noþ*er*

change his beauty or polish him, not by any means. The kinds that have been found have been borne in gold. The lapidary tells us that God gave many fair virtues and graces to the diamond, so that if a man bears it in strength and virtue, it keeps him from grievance, illusions and temptations, and from venom. Also it keeps the bones in the limbs whole, so much so that you will not fall off a horse or other beast except when the bone will be left whole, when someone bears it in purity of life. Also it defends against the dread that comes by night; and it does away heavy wrath and lechery; and it keeps a man in the same position as he finds himself, as to worth, understanding, value, riches – and enriches him in value, in riches and in goods, and he will not be made less; and he will be at little expense if he bears it in purity. A diamond is of great value for men of no understanding to look at, and it defends him from his enemies; and whoever bears it will love God more; also it keeps a man's seed within the womb of his wife, and it helps the child and keeps the child's limbs whole. The books tell us that if a woman is with child it must be borne on the left side. And whoever wants to prove his virtue must have it of true being, or of gift, and he will be whole and holy who bears this stone in purity; and it is mostly borne on the left side of a man or þinge may perse him, but with þe hote blode of a gote buke.

woman, and then he has virtue. Also this stone is not made with iron or steal and no other thing may pierce him, except the hot blood of a goat.

60. [Diadochus]

Diadose is a stone which is pale, & he is found in water, & he is gode to avoid deuelis, & he þreyeþ away mych derknes; and if it be set to a ded man he leseþ his kynd. And þis stone is lyk to berell. Diadosus is a ston riall & bry3t as berell; & it is able to haue answeres of fendes, for exceteþ fendes & fanta3ies; and if it hap þat it towche a ded man, it leseþ his vertu, for that ston hateþ a ded man, & he is scoymes of þinge þat is ouercom with deþe, as it seyd in bokes.

Diadochus is a stone which is pale, and he is found in water, and he is good for avoiding devils, and he drives away much darkness; and if it touches a dead man he loses his kind. And this stone is similar to beryl. The stone Diadochus is kingly, and as bright as beryl; and it is able to give answers of fiends, for it excites fiends and fantasies; and if it happens that it touches a dead man, it loses his virtue, for that stone hates a dead man, and he is squeamish of a thing that is overcome by death, as it is said in books.

61. [Dionisius]

Dionisa is a stone þat is blake as he schineþ as a riede stencellettes; & þis in clen water tride[101] mak wyne brene, & so with þe sauour of þis stone all dronkenes gooþe away; & all þe vater schall sauore of þe wyne by vertu of þis ston.

Dionisius is a stone that is as black and he shines with sparkles like a reed; and tested in pure water, this makes wine burn, and so with the savour of this stone all drunkenness goes away; and all water will taste of the wine by virtue of this stone.

---

[101] Evans and Serjeantson read 'tri[bl]e'.

62. [Pyrite]

Diodoma is a sto[n] formed square & it haþe coler of siluer. Men fynde in þe grauel of þe see.

Pyrite is a stone of square shape and it has the colour of silver. Men find it in the gravel of the sea.

63. [Liparea]

Disparea is a ston whiche is found in libia, & his kynde such þat all hunttyng comeþ which þat is lykyng to him. And þat bereþ þis stone may take þer-of ynowȝe, such vertu haþe þis ston.

Liparea is a stone which is found in Libya, and his kind is such that all things hunted come which desire him. And whoever bears this stone make take enough of them, such virtue has this stone.

64. [Diadochus]

Deadotes is a ston þat is lyke berrell. Yf þu wolt preve him in þy mowþe, þy mowþe schal bren but þu ~~but~~ put him owte þe rader. He þat bereth þis ston, þer schall no fantasie ouercom him. Also yf þis ston towche a ded body þris, this body schall aryse & mowe by vertu of þis ston, but he schall not speke neyþer doe. And if þu wilt þu mayst comaund what deuel of hel þu wilt & þe devel schal do no man harme. Þis ston may not often be nempned, for a man schal neuer dye whiles þis ston is vpon him.

Diadochus is a stone that is like beryl. If you want to prove him in your mouth, your mouth will burn unless you put him out instead. Whoever bears this stone, no fantasy will overcome him. Also if this stone touches a dead body three times, this body will arise and move by virtue of this stone, but he will neither speak nor act. And if you want, you may command whichever devil of hell you want and the devil will do no man harm. This stone may not often be obtained, for a man will not die while this stone is on him.

65. [Daphnaeum]

Diaffinian is a stone & it is like berell, redyssh, palyssh; he þat bereþ þis ston schall neuer have [fol. 7v] harme of nyȝt of no temtacion of deuel, ne he schall

Daphnaeum is a stone that is like beryl, reddish, palish; he who bears this stone will never come to harm by night by any temptation of the devil, nor will he ever have neuer haue þe blody mensyone ne þe palsey whiles he bereþ þis ston vpone him.

the bloody flux or the palsy while he bears this stone on him.

66. [Dionisius]

Dianya is a ston, & he is blak & haþe redyssh schynyng. Yf þu wil make wyne or all or water, it makeþ gode sauor to drynke; and grynde þis ston & put it in þe wyne or ale or water, & anoon it schall make þe licor of good sauour to drynke & doþe no harme.

Dionisius is a stone that is black and has a reddish shine. If you want to make wine or ale or water, it makes a good taste to drink; and grind this stone and put it in the wine or ale or water, and soon it will make the liquor of a good taste to drink, and does no harm.

67. [Draconite]

Draconitidis is a stone, & it is in a dragones hed. Some men clepen him escarbuncle. He schyneþ clerly. Non oþer vertu knowe I not þat it haþ; but in-as-mych for it is clere, lordes putten it in here tresor to kepe.

Draconite is a stone that is in a dragon's head. Some men call him escarbuncle. He shines clearly. I do not know any other virtue that it has; but because it is clear, lords put it in their treasure to keep.

68. [Emerald]

Esmeraude is a ston þat ouerpasseþ al þe grennesse of grenhede; and þe bokes seyne vs þat þe esmeraude & þe prames ben growyng togeders; and þe esmeraude comeþ owte of þe lond of tyre by a water of paradis. Nero haþe a myrrour of þis ston wherein he loked, & he wyst by þe vertu of þis stone al þat he wole seke or deseyre. It encresseþ ryches & makeþ word of man dredfull. Also is myche worþe aȝens þe gowte & aȝens tempest &

Emerald is a stone that surpasses all of the greenness of green things; and the books tell us that the emerald and the prasina grow together; and the emerald comes out of the land of Tyre by a river of paradise. Nero had a mirror of this stone in which he looked, and he knew by the virtue of this stone all that he sought or desired. It increases riches and makes the word of man feared. Also it is very valuable against the gout and against tempest and against aȝenes lechery, & it is gode souerenly for þe syȝte to beholdyn. Wit it wel, he þat bereþ it vpone him þe more he schal led his body in clennes, & þe les to loue vnclennes boþe of body & soule, & he schall haue þe mor loue to þinke one his soule, & þe more to loue clene beryng, & þe mor to loue gode workys. Also þis ston bereþ him fro tempest. God himself ȝaue such vertu þerto, and þe beyble seyþe þat þe esmeraude was the trid ston named of god vpone þe brest of aaron. Seint Iohne seyþe in þe apocalyps þat he sawe þe emeraude þe iiij stone vndere þe verry kyngdom. Also þer is a maner of beestes cleped gryffonnes þat kepen þe emaraudes vpone þe flod of paradyse in þe lond of syre; & þe bestes han iiij fete & ij wyngis; þe body befor & wynges ben in þe maner of an egle, & behynde [in] maner of a lion; and þer bene a maner of folk þat ben cleped acropolis, & þey han but oo ye in þe medys of þe forhed; & þese comen to seke þe emerawde all armede one þe water & taken him, & þe bestes beforseyd comen rennynge & flying, & wold take þe aropoles by here power & mych angwyssh hem, & egre ben to tak hem, but þey ben armed, þey may do hem no harme to tak hem.

lechery, and it is a sovereign remedy for the sight to behold. Understand well that he who bears it on him very frequently should conduct his body in purity, and should love impurity less, both of body and soul, and he will have more love to think on his soul, and more love for pure conduct, and more love for God's works. Also this stone protects him from tempest. God himself gave such virtue to it, and the Bible says that the emerald was the third stone named by God on the breast of Aaron. St John says in the Apocalypse that he saw the emerald as the fourth stone under the very kingdom. Also there is a kind of beasts called griffins that keep the emeralds on the river of paradise in the land of Syria; and the beasts have four feet and two wings. The body in front and the wings are in the shape of an eagle, and at the back in the shape of a lion; and there is a kind of people that are called cyclopes, and they have only one eye in the midst of the forehead; and these come to seek to seek the emerald all armed on the river and take him, and the aforesaid beasts come running and flying, and would take the cyclopes by their power and greatly hurt them, and are eager to take them, but they being armed they may do them no harm to take them.

69. [Bloodstone]

Elitropia is a ston, & is of scuch kynde, yf a man put in a vessel ful of water aȝens þe sone it schal make þe sone rede & in a lytel tyme, & he schall make þe vessel to cast owte þe water as it rey it reyneþ, and profiteþ myche to him þat bereþ it. Hit ȝeveþ a man gode fame, & also it stancheþ blode, also it is gode aȝens venymes & fylþes; and who þat takeþ þe erbe clepid elytrepie & þe charme þat longeþ þerto, & if he put it with þe ston, he schall mow go where he will. Þys ston comeþ owte of ethiope & egypte & of auffryk, as it were blody. Þys ston is gode befor many oþer stones; for god ȝafe him þat vertu & strenge, þat þe man þat setteþ him in a pleyn vessel & in clen water aȝens þe sone, as it is befor seyd; þe cause is þat he is apopred to þe clypsse; also who þat bereþ him schal be of gret purchese, & he bereþ a man in gret helpe, **[fol. 8r]** & makeþ a man to be of gret renoun. And some men seyne þat he is sumwhat like to þe emaraude; & he is cebled with red seyinctes; & he is a-luged to clyppsse, and he schall make þe eyr troble & reyne; and he makeþ gret d[i]unaciouns & gode fame.

Somme men seyne þat þis stone is som-what lyke to smaragdus, but he is not so grene, but grene

Bloodstone is a stone that is of such a kind that if a man puts it in a vessel of water against the sun it will make the sun red within a short time, and he will make the vessel cast out water as it rains, and is of much profit to him who bears it. It gives a man a good reputation, and also it staunches blood, also it is good against venoms and infections; and he who takes the herb called heliotrope and the charm that belongs to it, and puts it with the stone, he will more greatly go where he wants. This stone comes out of Ethiopia and Egypt and Africa, as though bloody. This stone is good, above many other stones, for God gave him that virtue and strength, so that if a man sets him in a plain vessel and in pure water against the sun, as was said before. The cause is that he corresponds to the eclipse; also, whoever bears him will be of great gain, and he brings in great help for a man, and makes a man to be of great renown. And some men say that he is somewhat similar to the emerald; and he is marked with red bands; and he is aligned to eclipses, and he will make the air cloudy and full of rain; and he makes great divinations and good reputation.

Some men say that this stone is somewhat similar to emerald, but he is not as green, but green veins veynes spreyng owte of him, redyssh like dropis of blode. And some mene seyne þat he is founde in a asse hede; for þis ston elitropia makeþ þe asse blynd. And whose bereþ þis stone schall neuer be blynde, & his syȝt schall neuer fayle him. Also towche a wounde with þis ston & þe wounde schall neuer rote; also wasse þis ston in wyne, & he schal neuer haue þe iawndyse. Þis ston makeþ fayr weder & cler, & he haþe many mo vertues. Also Ised seyþe þat þis ston discerneþ þe foly of enchaunthementes, & of wyches þat haue lykyng in pryde of her owne wondres þat þey begyle men with wondres þat þey worchin, as it is befor seyd. Also þat þis stone is gode & commendabyle for it stancheþ blode & putteþ away wenym, and he þat bereþ þis ston may not be begyled. Also þis elitropia is gren, & spreynede with red droppes & waynes as colour of blode, & haþe þe name & effecte & doynge of ecclypsse of þe sonne, as it is befor seyde.

spring out of him, reddish like spots of blood. And some men say that he is found in an ass's head; for this stone bloodstone makes the ass blind. And whoever bears this stone will never be blind, and his sight will never fail him. Also touch a wound with this stone and the wound will never rot; also wash this stone in wine, and he will never have the jaundice. This stone makes fair and clear weather, and he has many more virtues. Also Isidore says that this stone discerns the folly of enchantments, and of witches who enjoy the pride of their own wonders, by which they beguile men with the wonders they work, as aforesaid. Also this stone is good and commendable, for it staunches blood and puts away venom, and he who bears this stone may not be beguiled. Also this bloodstone is green, and sprinkled with red spots and veins like the colour of blood, and has the name and effect and action of eclipsing the sun, as aforesaid.

Nam si iungatur eius de nomine herbe / Carmine legitime verbeque sacrata potenti / Subtrait humanis occlis quem cunque gerentem.

For if his name is joined concerning the name of the herb [heliotrope] with a lawful song and powerful sacred words, it takes eyes away from men whoever wears it.

70. [Aetites]

Etite, de egle, is a ston & haþe many vertues. If a man will þe

Aetites, the eagle, is a stone that has many virtues. If a man wills harme, put þis ston vndyre his dish or in his disshe which he schal ete of, & he schall ete no mete whil þat ston is þer. Also he is gode for wymmen þat trauelyng with child. Also he makeþ a man riche & kynde. Also som men seyn þat þis ston etite is lyk to lynen cloþe wytest; & with-in him þer is anoder ston þat is blake. Þe egle getteþ[102] him in þe este & swoloweþ him, & when he will byeld his neste he leveþ him in a corner of his nest. Than dar no oder fowle cum to his neste, for þey wene þat egle be in his neste. If a man be aferde of poison of mete or drynke, lete þis ston towche þe mete or drynke viij tymes & it schall neuer do him harme. Also yf þis ston be bounden to a womens lefte arme in trauelynge sche schall be delyuerd withoute payne. Also dias seyþ þe vertu of þis ston: it makeþ a man sobre, & it encresseþ riches & loue, and he[l]peþ to victory & fauour, & letteþ & withstondeþ þe fallyng of him þat han þe fallyng yuell; and if a man haue suspecien of venym be in þe mete tak þis ston & ley it vnder his mete, & if þe venym be in þe mete he schal not swallow þe mete whilis þis ston is þer-in, & if þe ston be tak away he schal not tary to swolow þat mete, as Ised seyþe.

harm against you, put this stone under the dish he will eat from, and he will eat no meat while that stone is there. Also he is good for women who are labouring with child. Also he makes a man rich and kind. Also some men say that this stone aetites is the whitest, similar to linen cloth; and within him there is another stone that is black. The eagle gets him in the east and swallows him, and when he wants to build his nest he leaves him at the corner of his next. Then no other bird dares to come to his nest, for they understand the eagle is in his nest. If a man is afraid of poison in meat or drink, let this stone touch the meat or drink eight times and it will never do him harm. Also If this stone is bound to a woman's left arm in labour she will be delivered without pain. Also Dioscorides tells the virtue of this stone: it makes a man sober, and it increases riches and love, and helps to victory and favour, and prevents and withstands the falling of him who has the falling sickness; and if a man suspects venom take this stone and lay it under his meat, and if the venom is in the meat he will not swallow the meat while the stone is on it, and if the stone is taken away he should not delay in swallowing that meat, as Isidore says.

---

[102] Evans and Serjeantson read 'setteþ'

71. [Spinel Ruby]

Epistidio is a ston þat is precious, & it is seid þat it is rede; & he is gode for cold & he is gode for fruytes in þe erþe & for bredis, & he is god also for hayle & frostes, þat þu put him agaynst þe sonne. Also he makeþ branches as feyre. Also he makeþ al dowtable þinges Iput into sikernes.

Spinel ruby is a stone that is precious, and it is said that it is red; and he is good for cold and he is good for fruits in the earth and for breeding, and he is good also for for hail and frosts, if you put him against the sun. Also he makes branches like fire. Also he makes all doubtful things to be put into certainty.

72. [Hexacontalithos]

Exacontalito is a ston of sexti colours. Þis ston makeþ myche þe strenge of a lytel mane. And þis ston is founde amonge þe trogocdotes [fol. 8v] in þe contrey of libie.

Hexacontalithos is a stone of sixty colours. This stone makes the strength of a little man much. And this stone is found among the troglodytes in the country of Libya.

73. [Aetites]

Egestes is a ston þat is founde in þe contre of archade. Þis stone haþe þe color of yerne; & anoþer suche þer is þat is þe female; and whene sche conceyueþ, sche conceyueþ anoder stone. Þe vertu is more worþe to wymmen trauelynge in child-beryng, for sche schal þe soner be delyuerd.

Aetites is a stone found in the country of Arcadia. This stone has the colour of iron; and there is another kind that is female; and when she conceives, she conceives another stone. The virtue is of more value to women labouring childbirth, for she will be delivered soon.

74. [Enhydro]

Enydros is a stone & droppeþ away, & mylteþ note, & it is neuer þe lesse, & is always swetyng; & he is not wele grete, and he is founde in arabie in þe rede see, & he haþe senblaunt of cristall. Yf a

Enhydro is a stone which drips but does not melt, and it is never smaller, and is always sweating; and he is not very great, and he is found in Arabia and in the Red Sea, and he resembles crystal. If a man hold þis stone in þe sone-beme, it scheweþ to a man all þe colors of þe reynbowe. Enydros, þat stone, wepeþ alwaye as it were by sprenging of a ful well with droppyng teres, & welleþ always. And þerto it is seyd þat it is hard to tell þe cause þerof. For if þe droppis were of þe substaunce of þe ston wellyng, whi is not þe ston lese & melteþ away; and if a þing deencreseþ & put not aȝens þat þing þat goeþ owte; but as it semeþ to me, it may be þat þe vertu of þe ston makeþ þe eyre þik þat is is nyȝt þerto, & tornet into water, & so it semet þat comeþ owte of þe ston, neuer-þe-lese it comeþ owte of þe substance of þe eyre þat is abowte þe ston.

man holds this stone in a sunbeam, it shows to a man all the colours of the rainbow. That stone enhydro always weeps, as if it were the spring of a full well with dropping tears, and wells up perpetually. And it is said that it is hard to tell the cause of this. For if the drops were of the substance of the welling stone, why does the stone not become smaller and melt away, if a thing decreases and does not make up for the thing that goes out? But it seems to me that it may be that the virtue of the stone condenses the air that is near it, and turns it into water, and so it seems that it comes out of the stone; however, it comes out of the substance of the air that is around the stone.

75. [Exebenus]

Exebenius is a stone, & he is whitest, & þe growne is lyk golde. If a woman be syke in her bely, take þis stone & grinde it, & let here drynk þe powder with wyȝte wyne & sche schall be hole.

Exebenus is a stone that is very white, and the base is like gold. If a woman is sick in her belly, take this stone and grind it, and let her drink the powder with white wine, and she will be whole.

76. [Hepatite]

Epetites is a stone redyssh sum-what in schynyng, & if þu willt preue him holde þis ston in boylyng water, & þe water waxe colde by vertu of þis stone; also preue him, holde þis stone aȝens þe sonne, & owte of þe ston schall springe oute rayes aȝens þe soon. Also he is gode for women þat

Hepatite is a stone somewhat reddish in sheen, and if you want to prove him hold this stone in boiling water, and the water will grow cold by the virtue of this stone. Also to prove him, hold this stone against the sun, and rays will spring out of the stone against the sun. Also he is good for

44

trauelyng w*ith* child, and for wykkyd wormes & wicked te*m*pestes; and if a ma*n* may not do his will with a woma*n*, take þ*is* sto*n* & bynde it vpon*e* the reynes & he schall do what he will. Also it doþe away wordely wraþ. Al d*is* seyþe Ised & dias.

women labouring with child, and for wicked worms and wicked tempests; and if a man may not do his will with a woman, take this stone and bind it upon the kidneys and he will do what he wants. Also it does away worldly wrath. All this say Isidore and Dioscorides.

77. [Excoleritos]

Excoleritos is a litel ston, for it disteyned & dyue*r*sed w*ith* fowrty colo*r*s, & it is full bry3t, and þ*at* bry3t*n*es makeþ me[*n*] þ*at* loken þ*er*-on for to quake; and þ*is* ston is fonde in libie amo*n*ge þe trogodites.

Excoleritos is a little stone, for it is distinguished and made diverse by forty colours, and it is very bright; and that brightness makes men who look upon it quake; and this stone is found in Libya among the troglodytes.

78. [Yellow Ochre]

Firigins is a ston, & it haþe ve*r*tues of schyny*n*g oþ*er* colo*ur*. Þ*is* ston is gode if it be dro*n*kyne w*ith* sauen for þe gowte; also it is gode for to ber*e* abowte for þe palsey.

Yellow ochre is a stone that has the virtue of shining other colours. This stone is good if it is drunk with savin juniper for the gout; also it is good to carry about for the palsy.

79. [Fumonius]

Fimionis is a ston, & he þ*at* bereþ hi*m* þ*er* schal neu*er* no venym do hi*m* harme, ne he schal not be longe i*n* drede, ne no vnkend aue*n*t*ur* schal come to hi*m*; also yf he begyn eny gode þynge he schal mak a gode ende; also he schal not haue no wraþe, ned dred, ne no*n* anoye of lord ne lady. Also he þ*at* bereþ þ*is* ston schal neuer be brent; also he schall neu*er* be

Fumonius is a stone, and he who bears him will never be harmed by venom, nor will he not be in dread for long, nor will any unexpected adventure come to him. Also if he begins any good thing he will make a good end of it; also he will not have any wrath or dread or any annoyance of lord or lady. Also he who bears this stone will never be burnt; also he will never wonded ne hurte. Þese vertues & many mo þis ston haþe.

be wounded or hurt. These virtues and many more this stone has.

80. [Fedus]

Fedus is a ston for medecine. If it be grounden to small pouder, tak of þat pouder & womans mylke & medel him well togeder, so þat be of a man child, & wash þe sore yen wel þer-with, & þey schall be hole; and if eny body haue [fol. 9r] yuell in his [illeg.] take þe \l/ mylke of a schepe þat was a lambe þe same ȝere & þe pouder of þis ston, so þat he be a masculyn schepe & be wyȝt of schyne; let him drynke þat is potagre of þis medecyne & he schal be hole; but he muste drynke a lytell at onys for hys brayn; If he drynke mekel at ones, his brayne will fayle him.

Fedus is a stone for medicine. If it is ground to fine powder, take that powder and a woman's milk and mix them well together (and let it be milk for a man child) and wash the sore eyes well with it, and they will be whole. And if anyone has disease in his [illeg.] take the milk of a sheep which was a lamb in the same year and the powder of this stone (he should be a male sheep and shining white); let him who has the gout drink of this medicine and he will be whole; but he must drink a little at once for his brain. If he drinks a lot at once, his brain will fail him.

81. [Fensite]

Fensites is a stone, & is rede. Þe man or woman þat bereþ þis ston vpone hir ryȝt arme, þer schall neuer no wraþe of no maner man do him harme, so þat he be in clen leuyng & þe ston haue his kynde.

Fensite is a stone that is red. The man or woman who bears this stone upon their right arm, the wrath of no kind of man will never do him harm, provided he lives in purity of life and the stone has his kind.

82. [Florendanius]

Florendanius is a ston of many vertues & fulti[103] coloris. Yf eny body hange þis ston abowte his neke it helpeþ an euell þat is

Florendanius is a stone of many virtues and many colours. If anybody hangs this stone around his neck it helps an evil that is

---

[103] Evans and Serjeantson read 'ful[v]i'.

cleped arthetica. Also ȝ[e]f þis stone be holden hard in a mannes hand, a schall bren his honnde, & þerfor þu must smartly towche him.

called arthritis. Also if this stone is held firmly in a man's hand, it will burn his hand, and therefore you must touch him quickly.

83. [Jet]

Gagatis, þat is gete. He groweþ in a contrey þat men clepen licio, & it recembleþ myche to þe ademant; & faylet but lytell but þe best in þe world is in þe world is in breteyn maior, þat now is clepid ynglond. Þat ston is blake, schynyng, lyȝt & playn, & he is of many vertues; and when he is chafed by rubbyng or by fretyng it draueþ to him þe strees þat ben abowte him; and it brenneþ in water; & it is gode to ber to him þat haþe swellyng in sckyn or in flessh as a man þat is founded. Þe powder of him ywassh in a litel water clenseþ a man is teeþ & makeþ him faste. When a man brenneþ it & he haue þe gowte, anone as he feleþ þe odor & þe smell þerof þe gowte goeþ away. Also bren him, & þe smell þerof dreueþ away edders; & myche it worþe to him þat han her wombe ouerturned. And it fordoeþ wiche craft & charmes; also it dispreveþ maydenhede; also yf a woman trauell of child, of a drynk of þe water þat it haþe leye yne iij dayes & iij nyȝtes smertly sche schall be delyuerd with þe grace of gode. Also yf a man or woman may not pise for þe ston, take þe powder of geete & drynke it

Gagatis, that is, jet. He grows in a country that men call Lycia, and it greatly resembles diamond; and that which is in Great Britain, which is now called England, fails just a little to be the best in the world. That stone is black, shining, light and plain, and he is of many virtues; and when he is chafed by rubbing or by polishing it draws to him the straws that are around him; and it burns in water, and it is good for him to bear him who has swelling in the skin or flesh as a man who is affected by the glanders. The powder of him, washed in a little water, cleanses a man's teeth and makes them fast. When a man burns it and he has the gout, as soon as he senses the odour and the smell thereof the gout goes away. Also burn him, and the smell thereof drives away adders; and it is of much value to her who has her womb overturned. And it prevents witchcraft and charms; also it proves virginity; also if a woman is labouring with child, let her quickly drink of the water that it has lain in three days and three nights and she will be delivered with the grace of God. Also if a man or woman may not piss lewke-warme w*ith* red wyn*e* or w*ith* swete cowes mylke, & he schall pise anoo*n* & þe ston schal al to brek. Also he is good for þe fowle yuell; let hi*m* sauo*ur* to þe geete when it is brent. Also it is good to a ma*n* or a woma*n* yf þ*ey* bled byneþe, forþe tak a pan*e* w*ith* quyk colis, & let þe seke sitte bar*e* aboven clear iij dayes arow*e*, it schall stanche. Also who bereþ þ*is* ston abowte his nek, þ*er* schall no serpent do hi*m* harme. Also w*ith* þ*is* ston and a erbe þ*u* mi3test tie þe wildest beest in þe forest þ*at* he schold nat meve. Also þe fumusite þerof exciteþ me*n*strua if it is w*ith*draw by eny happe. Also it is seyd þ*at* it swageþ ache in þe wo*m*be, or yf þe stomake be torned by eny way. Also it helpcþ her þ*at* is tr*a*velyng of child. Ised seyþ of þ*is* ston*e* it wole bren*e* in wat*er*, & it is qwe*n*ched w*ith* oyle, & þ*at* is a wonder þyng.

because of the stone, take the powder of jet and drink it lukewarm with red wine or with sweet cows' milk, and he will soon piss and the stone will also break. Also he is good for the foul evil; let him smell the jet when it is burnt. Also it is good for a man or a woman if they bleed beneath; take out a pan with live coals, and let the sick person sit naked above them for three full days in a row; it will staunch. Also whoever bears this stone around his neck, there will no serpent do him harm. Also with this stone and a herb you may bind the wildest beast in the forest, so that he may not move. Also the fumes thereof excite the menstrual cycle if by any chance it stops. Also it is said that it assuages ache in the womb, or if the stomach is turned in any way. Also it helps her who is labouring with child. Isidore says of this stone that it will burn in water, and it is quenched with oil, and that is a wondrous thing.

84. [Gerachite]

Gerastie is a ston*e* of blac*is* color, & it is of gret price. Yf it be wasshe, put i*n*to a ma*n*nes mowþe vpon*e* his tonge, þ*at* yf a-noþ*er* ma*n* þynke eny þyng of hi*m* he schall known his þou3t anoon*e*. And yf a ma*n* wyl know his v*er*tu, anoy*n*t his body w*ith* hony or mylke, & set himself þ*er* as be*n* many fleyes, & put þ*is* ston i*n* his mowþe, & þ*er* **[fol. 9v]** scall no

Gerachite is a stone of blackish colour, and it is of great price. If it is washed, put it into a man's mouth, on his tongue; then if another man thinks anything about him he will soon know his thought. And if a man wants to know his virtue, let him anoint his body with honey or milk, and set himself where there are many flies, and put this stone in his

48

fley euer ney3 him. And some men callen þis stone genardus.

mouth, and no fly will ever come near him. And some men call this stone *genardus*.

85. [Gagatromaeus]

Gagantruels is a stone, & is lik to þe skyn of a kyd. Þe princes beren þe ston with hem into batayl, ase þe chasen away her enmyes. Ercules ascaped all his enemyis & many perelles by vertu of þis stone.

Gagatromaeus is a stone that is similar to the skin of a kid. Princes bear the stone with them into battle, and it chases away their enemies. Hercules escaped all his enemies and many perils by virtue of this stone.

86. [Nitrate of Lime]

Galactida is a ston, & is myche lyke to asshen; & yf he be dronke in mylke he restoreþ mylke; but it most be vsed befor mete; & sche þat bereþ it is good for child-berynge. And it kep schepe fro scabbys, & makeþ full of mylk. Þis stone galactides haþe many dyuers names. Some clepen him gracitem & egipcis smaragdene, & his ry3t name is galactida. Also men clepen him ganancten & fenichom & letorgone & we clepen him oblianus. He þat bereþ þis stone, his will schall be fulfelled. If þu wilt know þis ston, it smelleþ lyke [*illeg.*] hony; & grynde him to powder & he schalle waxe whi3t. And if a woman drynk þe pouder sche schall hawe plente of mylke; and yf and yf þe stone be persyd and hanggyd abowt her neke that is with childe, sche schall be deliuerid anon withowt any perell. And if þe child be scabbyd, washe

Nitrate of lime is a stone that is very similar to ashes; and if he is drunk in milk he restores milk; but it must be used before meat; and she who bears it is good for childbearing. And it keeps sheep from scabies, and makes full of milk. This stone nitrate of lime has many different names. Some call him gracite and Egyptian emerald, and his proper name is *galactida*. Also men call him *ganancten* and *fenichom* and litharge, and we call him *oblianus*. Whoever bears this stone, his will will be fulfilled. If you want to know this stone, it smells like [*illeg.*] honey; and grind him to powder and he will turn white. And if a woman drinks the powder she will have plenty of milk; and if the stone is pierced and hung around the neck of her who is with child, she will soon be delivered without any danger. And if the child has scabies, wash him with þe mylke of a schepe or þe sone ryse, and he schall be hole. And if her teþe be sor, wesh hem with þe mylke. And yef thou bere þe ston þu schalte be glade, and þu schalte neuer dyy in batell nor neuer be a-ferryd. Also yef a woman may not be deliuerid, tye þe stone to here lefte thee with a þerde of wole of schepe. This galaxide is swete in taste and sauoure; yf he be smyttyn, þer will come owt ~~mylk~~ a maner of swete mylke, as ysaidre sayd. This stone iclowsid distrowbillyth þe wyt; and yef hit be bore abowte þe neke hit makyth brestes full of mylke. And yef hee be medillyd with watter & salte and spronge abowte þe feldes, then þe schepe schall be full of mylke. Also hee schall clense sckabbys as diases. And yef hit be bownd to þe theys hit makyþ yessy byrth.

him with sheeps' milk before sunrise, and he will be whole. And if their teeth are sore, wash them with the milk. And if you bear this stone you will be glad, and you will never die in battle nor be afraid. Also if a woman may not be delivered, tie the stone to her left thigh with a thread of sheep's wool. This nitrate of lime is sweet in taste and smell; if he is struck, there will come out a sort of sweet milk, as Isidore says. This stone enclosed unclouds the under-standing, and if it is borne around the neck it makes breasts full of milk. And if he is mixed with water and salt and sprinkled around the fields, then the sheep will be full of milk. Also he will cleanse scabies, as Dioscorides says. If if is bound to your thighs it makes easy birth.

87. [Garsius]

Garsius is acowntyd amonge þe stonys, and hit is not lefe, for hit haþ no prophete but that hee is grene. Also þer bene odere that haþe small venys blodinth. The þirde maner haue iij maners and be figuryd whit. Isid saiþe þis stone schall neuer be hotte with fyre and dias saiþe the same.

Garsius is counted among the stones, and it is not beloved, for it has no property, except that he is green. Also there are others that have small bloody veins. The third kind have three sorts and are patterned with white. Isidore says that this stone will never be hot with fire and Dioscorides says the same.

88. [Chalazias]

Galcido uel gelacid is a ston that is like þe Addemand, for he haþe

Chalazias or gelacid is is a stone that is similar to diamond, for he noo vertu to noo medisyne, for he is colde as anny yse and þerfor he is put to noo medisyne ne in l[e]se a manere as do oder stones for he will not be schafyd be noo fyre.

has no virtue to any medicine, for he is as cold as any ice and therefore he is used in no medicine, in no less a manner as other stones for he will not be ignited by any fire.

89. [Hyena]

Hieme is a stone þe wiche a best berethe, the wiche is clepide hieme, in þe bale of his ye; this stone, as holde autors seyne schall make a man diuinable, for yef [fol. 10r] a man haue it vnder his tonge, so that his mowth be clen wassh, for then he haþe his strengeþ. Also yf he be bore, þis ston, vndyr his tonge, he schall sey þe soþe to what man þat askeþ him.

Hyena is a stone which a beast bears, which is called hyena, in his eyeball; this stone, as old authors say, will give a man powers of divination, for if a man has it under his tongue, provided that his mouth is washed clean, he will then have his strength. Also if he bears this stone under his tongue he will say the truth to whatever a man asks of him.

90. [Macedony]

Macedone is a stone þat yf women ber him if sche trauayl of child sche schall neuer be delyuerd til þat stone be tak awaye.

Macedony is a stone that if a woman bears him if she is labouring with child, she will never be delivered until that stone is taken away.

91. [Herinaceus]

Herimacius is a stone, & his color is in maner lyke þe mayle of an hawke; þe vertues of him can I not fynde ʒet.

Herinaceus is a stone whose colour is in a way like the mail of a hawk; the virtues of him I cannot find yet.

92. [Hispania]

Hispannen est gemma quae reperitur in littoribus hispaniensis occeainis ignee & perlucede.

Hispania is a fiery and translucent gem which is found in the ocean coasts of Spain.

93. [Jasper]

Iaspes. Þer bene þer of \x/ xvij maners colours, & þey ben founde in well depe parties of þe wourdyll; but he þat is grene aȝens þe daye, he is godly, & when he is blake dropes he [is] lese worþe. And when it is dropped with rede & it is grene, & he schapyd after the old schape, he is lorde of all the iaspe; þis is þe moste precius Iaspe. Þes iaspes ben founde in many parteys of the world; þose bene here vertues: Iaspes is good aȝens all maner of wormes; and oone be stonge with wenym or any oder maner poysone, & he be brouȝt in eny maner stede as iaspe is, he schal choynde[104] anoon owte of color, and it schall stanche blode be resone of him þat haþe gode beleue, or of mensyone, or feuer, or dropsye; and whoso beholdeþ iaspe aȝens daye, he schall expounde dremes and also mych worþe to woman þat trauelyþ of child; if sche haue it vpone her sche schall þe soner be delyuerd. Iaspes kepethe a mane fro his aduersarys; and whoso bereþ him he most kepe clene lyfe. Þe bok telleþ vs þat þe goode iaspe is grene and moyses set þis ston in þe brest of arone. Sent Iohn seyþe in apocolyps þat he say in heuenly kyndome of ierusalem þat þe ferst fundament wase Iaspe. Þe grenest Iaspe is a caladone. He þat bereþ

Jasper. There are seventeen kinds of colours of it, and they are found in very deep parts of the world; but he who is green against the daylight, he is holy, and when he has blackish spots he is of less value. And when it is spotted with red and it is green, and he is shaped after the old shape, he is lord of all the jaspers: this is the most precious jasper. These jaspers are found in many parts of the world; these are their virtues. Jasper is good against all kinds of worms; and if someone is stung with venom or any other kind of poison, and if he is brought into any place where jasper is, he will soon change out of colour; and it will staunch blood by reason of him who has good belief, as well as menses, fever, or dropsy; and whoever beholds jasper against daylight, he will expound dreams and it is also very valuable to women who are labouring with child; and if she has it on her she will be delivered sooner. Jasper keeps a man from his adversaries; and whoever bears him must live a pure life. The book tells us that the good jasper is green, and Moses set this stone in the breast of Aaron. St John says in the Apocalypse that in the heavenly kingdom of Jerusalem the first foundation was jasper. The greenest jasper is caladony. He

---

[104] Evans and Serjeantson read 'choyn[g]e'.

þis stone schal nereuer dey in water, ne his enemy schal ouercomen him. A man schall let graue in þis stone yarmede, & a ȝewrd in his honde, with a stoole abowȝt his neke & a ȝerde þat schold be of be of olyuetre; & his vertu is gret in siluer þen in gold; also þer is one þat is a blak colour. And some seyn þat þe Iaspe is of xvij maner colours; & þat is blak is mor myȝt & worþe, & grener[105] of valew & of vertu for he comforteþ many men of fantome. Also Ised seyþ þat one of þe iaspes is fonde in þe hed of a edder which is clepid aspis; and þis ston iaspis is but lytell. Som men seyn þat it is a stone of wonder vertu; & þis stone is named after aspis. Dias seyþe þat þe best iaspis is founde in þe moyntens of sicia, & gripes kepen þis stone as þey don smaragdus.

who bears this stone will never die in water, no will his enemy overcome him. A man should engrave this stone armed, with a sword in his hand, with a stole about his neck and a staff that should be of olive wood; and his virtue is greater in silver than in gold; also there is one that is a black colour. And some say that the jasper is of seventeen kinds of colours; and that black is stronger and more valuable, and the greener kind is of value and virtue, for he comforts many men troubled by phantoms. Also Isidore says that one of the jaspers is found in the head of an adder which is called asp; and this stone jasper is only little. Some men say that it is a stone of wondrous virtue; and this stone is named after asp. Dioscorides says that the best jasper is found in the mountains of Scythia, and griffins keep this stone as they do emerald.

94. [Jacinth]

Iagunce is a ston, & is of many maners. Þe gret iacunce is rede & it is of gentyl maner & of gret vertu. It kepeþ a man trew, and it makeþ a man to beholden trew. Anoder Iagunce, & is of ȝelow colour, & it is called citri. Þes ij maners of iagunce ben of þes vertus, þat when a man putteþ him in his moweþ he makeþ a man riȝt

Jacinth is a stone that is of many kinds, the great jacinth is red and it is of gentle kind and of great virtue. It keeps a man true, and it makes a man see truly. Another jacinth is of yellow colour, and it is called citrine. These two kinds of jacinth have these virtues, that when a man puts him in his mouth he makes him very cold, and he

---

[105] Evans and Serjeantson read 'gre[t]er'.

cold, and he þat bereþ it vpon him may go into anoþer contre wiþowte dred, & he schal be worchipid in his oste howse; in al maner þyng þat he askeþ it resonable it schal not be hid fro him; & þis stone schal be put in golde. Some men seyne þat þer ben iij maner iagunces; þat one is full of geynes,[106] þat oþer ȝelow, þe þryd is pleyn; and þey comforteþ weyn suspeciose[107] & heuynes; & he is allmost as hard as adyamont; & he wol be bore in rynges or at a manes nyke, & þen he may go save wher he wolle. And some seyn þat **[fol. 10v]** he comeþ owte of yende þe mor. Also he is gode for medesyns. Al þes iagunce be red brownyssh, and þer [ben] iij maners of hem, þat oone is gryned, þat oder is ful of vaynes, þe þryd is pleyn. The tho maners of stones þu schalt preue hem in þe feyr, wil be cler & lyȝt; þe pleyn iacyuncte will suffre no feyr, but he is good to distroy a felone & to stanche blode, and yf þu pers him & binde him abowte þey naked flysh þer schal no tempest do þe harme, Þe ryȝt colour is as þe firmament þat makeþ þe daye, and þus þu schalt him knowe.

who bears it on him may go into another country without dread, and he will be honoured in his host's house; in all kinds of things he asks (if reasonable), it will not be hidden from him; and this stone should be set in gold. Some men say that there are three kinds of jacinths; that one is full of greyness, that another is yellow, and that the third is plain; and they comfort vain suspicions and heaviness; and he is almost as hard as diamond; and he should be borne in rings or at a man's neck, and then he may go safely wherever he wants. And some say that he comes out of the greater India. Also he is good for medicines. All these jacinths are red brownish, and there are three kinds of them; one is gritty; another is full of veins; the third is plain. The three kinds of stones, should you prove them in the fire, will be clear and light; the plain jacinth will endure no fire, but he is good to destroy a felon and to staunch blood, and if you pierce him and bind him around your naked flesh no tempest will do you harm. The right colour is like the firmament that makes the day, and this you will know him.

95. [Celidony]

Irunde is a stone & is founde in de wombe of a bryde þat men callen

Celidony is a stone that is found in the womb of a bird that men

---

[106] Evans and Serjeantson read 'g[r]eynes'.
[107] Evans and Serjeantson read 'suspecio[n]se'.

þe swallowȝe in englyssh; þe ȝonge briddys, while þey be in þe nest, þe wombe schall be kytte, & in þe mowþe ȝe schul fynde iij maners of stones, oon blak, anoþer redyssh, anoþer of diuers colours. Item celidonus est lapis palydus & fuscus & aliquantulum obscurus quasi perforetur; causas aduersatur, & virtutes conseruat, vt dicit albertus. Þat ston þat is blak is gode for sor yene, of what cause so þat it be, & it comforteþ þe syȝt. Þat oder þat is of dyuers colours is aȝens caduce men for to han or abowte her neck; it helpeþ þat he schal neuer haue it more. Also þis stone it makeþ scharp syȝt; and also drye it & make pouder of it, & it helpeþ þe squynacye. Also þe erbe with þe stone is profitable.

call the swallow in English; the womb of the song birds, while they are in the nest, should be cut open, and in the mouth you will find three kinds of stones, one black, another reddish, another of several colours. Item, celidony is a pale and dusky stone, and somewhat opaque as if perforated; it overturns causes, and preserves virtues, as Albert says. The stone that is black is good for sore eyes, from whatever cause, and it comforts the sight. The other one that is of several colours is against epileptic men to hang about their necks; it helps him never to have it again. Also this stone makes sharp sight; and also dry it and make powder from it, and it helps the quinsy. Also the herb with the stone is profitable.

96. [Jacinth]

Iacincte is a stone myche clyr, & it is of iij maners; þat oone is of violet colour, þe oder of red, þe iij color as [illeg.]. Al þes ben gode for medcyns, and þorowȝ her strengeþ and hir vertu þey done away al idel þowȝtes & hewynes; and who þat bereþ it vpon him, he may go savely wher he wole, and he schal be myche worchipid in all places. And he comeþ owte of þe mor Inde, & he wold be set in gold. Þis iacincet, as men seyne, he [is] blowȝ & grene of colour, þicke & derk as purpull colour; & he is lyke to þe reynbowe, & he is of such colour. Ised seyþ þis stone

Jacinth is a very clear stone, and it is of three kinds; one is of violet colour, the other red, the third colour like [illeg.]. All these are good for medicines, and through their strength and their virtue they do away all idle thoughts and heaviness; and whoever bears it on him may go safely where he wants, and he will be much honoured in all places. And he comes out of the greater India, and he should be set in gold. This jacinth, as men say, is blue and green in colour, as thick and dark as the colour of purple, and he is like the rainbow, and he is such a

55

þat is founde in ethiope is best, & is not to cler ne to dyme, but mene & temperat betwyx shynyng. And Ised seyþ þat ston schyneþ not always liche, for in cler wedyr he is cler before þe yene, & in derke wedder it is derke & dymme; also Ised seyþe in þe morun cold, if it is þerin. And it is most hard to graue yne, neuer-þe-lese it may be graue ynne & ywryten & ymarked with þe stone adamans. As ysed seyd þat þe stone iacincte is now blew, now redyssh, now purpill color, now briȝt blew; & þer ben iij maners of kyndes for ben citrin & some blew; but amonge shuch the blew is beste. Also þis ston is wondyrful, for confermeþ most to þe eyre, for in dym weddyr he is dym, & in cler wedder he is clere; and so þis ston haþe a syngler vertu, for it ȝefeþ gladnes & is contrary to malyncole qualite, & he haþe vertu of comfort, as it is seyd in þe kynd þerof. Iacinctus haþe vertu of comfort; & he doþe awaye al elyngenese & sorrow, & also veyne suspeciosnes, & withstondeþ dyuerse pestolens þat comen ofte of a corupte eyre; & it ȝeweþ strenge & vertu to membres & lyfe to þe synewis & ȝeveþ good sauor & swet & hollsom; & it lyke to þe saphur. Also dias seyþe, & al men þat treten of precious stones seyn, that þe iacinte is lyke þe saphur in color & substans, þe mor vertues he is; and such iacincte withstondeþ venymes, & is contrary to poysone, as dias seyþ; þer is a

colour. Isidore says that the stone that is found in Ethiopia is the best, and is neither too clear nor too dim, but shining in the middle and temperate between them. And Isidore says that the stone does not always shine in the same way, for in clear weather he is clear before the eyes, and in dark weather it is dark and dim. Also Isidore says it is cold in the morning, if it is in it. And it is very hard to engrave in; nevertheless it can be engraved and written upon and marked with the stone diamond. As Isidore says, that stone is now blue, now reddish, now purple in colour, now bright blue; and there are three kinds of which one is citrine, and some are blue; but among them the blue is the best. Also this stone is wonderful, for is conforms the most to the atmosphere; for in dim weather he is dim, and in clear weather he is clear, and so this stone has a singular virtue, for it gives gladness and is contrary to the melancholy quality, and he has the virtue of comfort, as it is said of the kinds thereof. Jacinth has the virtue of comfort, and he does away all melancholy and sorrow, and also vain suspicions, and withstands several pestilences that often come from corrupt air; and it gives strength and virtue to limbs and life to the sinews, and gives a good taste that is sweet and wholesome; and it is like the sapphire. Also Dioscorides says, and all men who treat of precious herbe of þe same name is lyk þerto in many þinges, þow it be not lyke in walew, as Ised seyþe.

stones say, that the more the jacinth is like the sapphire in colour and substance, the more virtuous he is; and such jacinth withstands venoms, and is contrary to poison, as Dioscorides says. There is a herb of the same name that is similar in many ways, though it is not not similar in value, as Isidore says.

97. [Jaspacates]

[fol. 11] Iapectes is a stone, & þer bene many of dyuers colours & of many maners; for he that bereþ þis ston vpone him he may wel goo in-to batayl & ouercom his aduersaryis, & it kepeþ a man riȝt hardy & ful of mych godnes.

Jaspacates is a stone, and there are many of several colours and of many kinds; for he who bears this stone on him may well go into battle and overcome his adversaries, and it keeps a man very bold and full of much goodness.

98. [Jacinth]

Iacinctornicta is a ston, & he is myche lyke to cristal; & if it towche a man is heer it waxiþ blak. Oþer vertues know I noon.

Jacinth is a stone that is very similar to crystal; and if it touches a man's hair it turns black. I do not know any other virtues.

99. [Quirine]

Iren is a stone, & it is haþe þese vertues. Take þis & ley it vpone a manis brest or woman brest sleping & þey schall tel al þat þey han doune. Also ber þis ston in þey purse, for it schal do awaye all fantasies in þe brayne. Yf þu wilt fynd þis stone, go to þe lampwynch neste whene he ley dyren,[108] & tak a glasse cuppe &

Quirine is a stone that has these virtues. Take this stone and lay it on a man's breast or a woman's breast while sleeping and they will tell all that they have done. Also bear this stone in your purse, for it will do away all fantasies in the brain. If you want to find this stone, go to the lapwing's nest when he lies therein, and take a

---

[108] Evans and Serjeantson (incorrectly) read 'leyd yren'.

ley it above þe nest & styk ij roddes on crose wyse above, & þe[n] will þe lapwynche fle to þe rede see & fete a ston, & towche þer-with þe glase cuppe, & þe coppe will breke & þe ston will fale doune into þe nest & so he bryngeþ forþe his bryddes. And þe ston haþe many mo vertues then I can tell.

glass cup and lay it above the nest, and stick two rods crosswise above, and then the lapwing will fly to the Red Sea and fetch a stone; and touch it with the glass cup, and the cup will break and the stone will fall down into the nest; and in this way he brings forth his birds. And the stone has many more virtues than I can tell.

100. [Indres]

Indres is a preciose stone þat þe raven feccheþ at þe red see or in ynde. Take þe stone & put it in a rynge, & þen take a lefe of laureal & wynd þe ryng þeryn, & towche þerwith feters or lokys & þey schall vndo. Also [tak] þe ston & put it in þey mowþe & þu schalt have vndyrstondyng of all langgages. Also þis ston putteþ awaye all wraþes & yre. Also he þat haþe þis ston abowte him he schall neuer fayle goode wyle þat he leueþ in þis worle. & þis ston is of many colors & rownde. And þus þu mayst have þis stone, go to þe raven is neste when he haþe leyþe & tak adowne þe eyerne & feþer him hard, & þen ber þyn to þe nest aȝen; & þe raven will fle to þe red see or in to ynde & fiche þis stone & [put] it amonge her eyrne stryng[109] it with his byle al abowte, & þe eyren schall waxe rawe, & so he brengeþ forþe his bryddys by wertu of þe ston.

Indres is a precious stone that the raven fetches from the Red Sea or in India. Take the stone and put it in a ring, and then take a leaf of laurel and wind it in the ring, and touch fetters or locks with it and they will undo. And take the stone and put it in your mouth and you will have understanding of all languages. Also this stone puts away all wrath and anger. Also he who has this stone about him will never lack good will as long as he lives in this world. And this stone stone is of many colours and round. And you way have this stone in this way: go to the raven's nest when he has laid, and take down the eggs and burden him hard, and then bear yours to the nest again; and the raven will fly to the Red Sea or into India and fetch this stone and put it among her eggs, stirring it all around with his beak, and the eggs will grow thin, and in this way he brings forth his birds by virtue of

---

[109] Evans and Serjeantson read 'st[y]ryng'.

this stone.

101. [Ipacon]

Ipacon e*st* lapis *qui* nascit*ur* in libia ad q*uem* cu*r*ru[n]t o*mn*es bestis tanq*uam* ad refugiu*m* & [*illeg.*] & [*illeg.*] ne nocea*nt* a*n*imali*a*.

Ipacon is a stone which is born in Libia, to which run all beasts as if to safety and [*illeg.*] lest the animals should do harm.

102. [Irachite]

Irachie is a ston; þe ma*n* þat bereþ hi*m* schal nat be bytten w*ith* fleyes, neyþer stonge w*ith* bene as Dias seyþe; & men suppoȝeþ it helpeþ aȝe*n*s veny*m*.

Irachite is a stone; the man who bears him will not be bitten by flies, neither stung by bees, as Dioscorides says; and men suppose it helps against venom.

103. [Molas]

Molas is a ston, & his v*er*tu is not but when mone is at full; he most scharply be draw vp & whe*n* þe sone schyneþ vpon*e* hi*m*, & then he takeþ is full v*er*tu.

Molas is a stone who has no virtue unless the moon is full; he must be drawn up sharply when the sun shines on him, and then he receives his full virtue.

104. [Lyngurium]

Ligurie is a stone of ynde fonden vpon þe flode þ*at* is cleped Quendis; & þer is a best wiche is cleped lynse, & he kepeþ & w*ith*holdeþ þ*is* stone wel depe i*n* his þrote for the gret v*er*tu þerof schuld nat cu*m* to vs. Þe bok*es* tellen vs þ*at* þer ben ma*n*y mane*r*s liguries, but þe best is he þ*at* haþe þe colo*r* of goldy. And also þer ben such þ*at* ben lyke þe color of

Lyngurium[110] is a stone of India found in the river that is called Quendis; and there is a beast which is called the lynx; and he keeps and withholds this stone very deep in his throat, so that the great virtue of it should not come to us. The books tell us that there are many kinds of lyngurium, but the best is he who has the colour of gold. And also there are some

---

[110] Both amber and tourmaline have been suggested as possible identifications of lyngurium (Walton (2001), p. 365).

mire, & some of þe color of encens; & som þer ben þat ben like þe color to ȝelow grenehed, & som of þe color of mylk; as a maister deuysed þat þer ij maners of topacie. Moyses seyþe vs þat þer ben some of þe color of Iagounce. Owr lorde ȝaue to þis ston many feyr vertues it heleþ þe iaundyse; & it restryneþ a man fro [*illeg.*] vices. Also he is god aȝens þe gowte, & it clenseþ a man of sorowes, & it helpeþ þe **[fol. 11v]** stomak. Ligure pleseþ a man þat is wraþfull, & gladeþ him; also he stancheþ þe blody menyson & þe bledyng membres. And þe bokes tellen vs þat þis ston is good to ladys, for þis ston schal make hem plesyng to her lordes. Also þis ston coleþ a man of gret hetes if it is put in his mowþe. Also who-so towcheþ a manes sor eyne, it schal dryue owte þe yuel & þe blode. And wite it well þat þis stone haþe be cleped by many oþer names, but owr autours clepeþ it ligurie. Moyses clepeþ þe best ox, & þe vertu of þis lymes telleþ vs Iob; þese lechores men aȝens þe lymes shold we haue þe vertu in vs þat sigifieþ chastite; also þe best befor seyd þat dyggeþ þe erþe to hid þe ston. The bible seyþe vs þat þis ston was pute in þe þryd corner in þe brest of arone. Also it helpeþ a mane of þe excesse & of þe meneson, & he amendeþ þe ache of þe stomak, & makeþ þe entrals of a man hole. Also Ised seyþ þat þer is a best þat is cleped lynx, & þe ston lygurius comeþ of þe

which are like the colour of myrrh, and some the colour of incense; and there are some that are like the colour of yellow greenhead, and some the colour of milk; as a master devised, there are two kinds of topaz. Moses tells us that there are some the colour of jacinth. Our Lord gave to this stone many fair virtues: it helps jaundice, and it restrains a man from [*illeg.*] vices. Also he is good against the gout, and it purifies a man of sorrows, and it helps the stomach. Lyngurium pleases a man who is angry, and gladdens him; also he staunches bloody menses and bleeding limbs. And the books tell us that this stone is good for ladies, for this stone will make them pleasing to their lords. Also this stone cools a man from great heat if it is put in his mouth. Also, whoever touches a man's sore eyes with it, it will drive out the evil and the blood. And understand well that this stone has been called by many other names, but our authors called it lyngurium. Moses calls the best kind ox, and Job tells us the virtues of these limbs. These lecherous men against the limbs should we have the virtue in us that signifies chastity; also the aforesaid beast who digs the earth to hide the stone. The Bible tells us that this stone was set in the third corner on the breast of Aaron. Also it helps a man with excess of blood and the bloody flux, and he heals stomach ache, beste, & it is gendryd in þe grauel of þe see of þe vryng of þe same best. Also he draweþ straw to himself.

and makes the entrails of a man whole. Also Isidore says that there is a beast that is called lynx, and the stone lyngurium comes from the beast, and it is produced in the gravel of the sea from the urine of the same beast. Also he draws straw to himself.

105. [Serpentine]

Lange serp[e]nt is of many colors, & he is of schap a tonge; but þis ston is broun, blak, & þe [*illeg.*] red aȝens þe mone, is þerin most vertu, & þefendeþ a mane fro venym, and yf a mane be poysened it kepeþ him; & þerfor þey put it in seluer befor kyngis & princes & befor oder gret lordes at her metes & drynkes. Þu myȝtes set þyn boþe in gold & in siluer; and men fynd him in many places in þe see grauel of þe gret bretone.

Serpentine is of many colours, and he is the shape of a tongue; but the stone which is brown, black, and [*illeg.*] red against the moon has within it the most virtue, and defends a man from venom, and if a man is poisoned it preserves him; and therefore they put it in a salver before kings and princes and before other great lords at their meat and drink. You may set yours both in gold and in silver, and men find him in many places in the sea gravel of Great Britain.

106. [Liparea]

Laparie is a ston, & he fonde of contreis of libie, & his kynd is mych of wyld bestes, for he is gode for hunters when þey have no hounde. For when he þat bereþ þis ston vpone him schal not not haþe in huntyng. Ised seyþe þe laparie comeþ owte of þe contre of cirtes. Þe propirte of þis ston, þat wild bestes comen to þe stones presense & beholden þerone; and for bestes þat may not be taked with hondes, þey taken & tollen him with þe syȝt & schynyng only

Liparea is a stone which is found in the country of Libya, and his kind is much for wild beasts, for he is good for hunters when they have no hound. For when he who bears this stone on him will not fail in hunting. Isidore says that liparea comes out of the country of Syrtis. The property of this stone is that wild beasts come into the stone's presence and look at it; and for beasts which may not be taken with hounds, they take and entice them with the sight and of þe laparia.   shining of liparea alone.

107. [Magnet]

Magnes is a stone þat is fonde among to maneris of folkes, þat one cleped trogadite, & oþer is cleped ynde; & in þat contre men fynd him, & he haþe þe color of yern. Delder þe enchanter vsed it myche, for he wist wel þat it helped mych to enchantemenes; and after him vsed it mych þe mervelows enchauntere Cierce, was a woman. Amonge all oþer experyinneces it is founde & knowen & it is soþe of a mane & of his wife, as it is seyd after in þe verses. Also yf a thefe enter into an howse for to stell, & yf he tak a quyk bronde of fyr & [illeg.]. Also þis ston makeþ loue betwen man & woman, & gyfeþ a man grace to spek sweetly; and yf a man [g]yf it to drynk in oyle to him þat haueþ þe dropsy it schal porge him. And þe powder is good for brenyng. Also whoso bereþ þis ston schal neuer be wroþe with his wyfe, ne þe wyfe with þe hosbone. Also he þat hath a felon, drynke þe powder þerof, & he schall be hole. Also yf a woman drynke þe powder þerof sche schal be baren; and yf a man drynke iiij tymes he schal lese his genetralis. And yf þu þrawe þe powder þerof in þe feyr, al þe men þat loken in þe feyr schal wene

Magnet is a stone that is found among two kinds of people; one is called troglodyte and the other Indian; and in that country men find him, and he has the colour of iron. Delder[113] the enchanter used it much, for he knew well that it helped much for enchantments; and after him the marvellous enchanter Circe, who was a woman, used it much. Among all other experiments, it is found and known, and it is true of a man and of his wife, as it is said afterwards in the verses. Also if a thief enters a house to steal, and if he takes a live brand of fire and [illeg.] Also this stone makes love between man and woman, and gives a man grace to speak sweetly; and if a man gives it to drink in oil to him who has the dropsy it will purge him. And the powder is good for burning. Also whoever bears this stone will never be angry with his wife, nor the wife with the husband. Also let him who has a morbid swelling drink the powder of it, and he will be whole. Also if a woman drinks the powder of it she will be barren; and if a man drinks four times he will lose his genitals. And if you throw the powder of it in the fire, everyone who looks in the fire will know

---

[113] Perhaps a corruption of the name of Telemus, son of Eurymus, the Cyclopean seer (*Odyssey* 9.509).

þat þe howse schal fal downe. Þis stone is fonden in þe see of ynde; þis is ryȝt gode to be set in a rynge aȝure. Also Isodre seyþ, þis magnete is a ston of ynde, colored somdel as yern; & it is fonde in Indea[111] amonge þe trogodites, & draweþ **[fol. 12r]** to himself yern; & it is founde in ynde, so þat it makeþ as it were a scheyne of yerne with ryngis, as Ised seyþe; þerfor in þe comen speche þis yerne is clepid quyk yerne. Þe myȝth & þe vertu þerof is so gret, as austen seyþe, þat ane a ston be sete vnder a vessel of gold or off brase or yerne set þervpone, by mouyng of þe stone þat is byneþe, yerne schall moue þat is aboue. Also it is seyd that þer is in anoþer contre in a tempill an ~~ȝis alone also it~~ \ymage/ of yerne, & it semeþ þat ymage hangeþ in þe eyre. And in ethiopa is anoþer maner of kynd of magnes þat forsakeþ yerne & dryueþ away fro it self. Also þe magnes draweþ þe eyrne in to a corner; & þe mor blew þe mor better he is. Also diascorides & lapidarie seyen þat þis ston reconcileþ & acordeþ lowe betwene men & her wyfes. Also it ȝeueþ grace & feyernes in speche & in worde. Also a drynke Imad of hony & of wyne it helpeþ þe dropsi & þe splen & þe fallyng yuel, & also for brenyng. Plata seyþe þat wyches vse namly of þis stone. Also þis stone magnes is

that the house will fall down. This stone is found in the sea of India; this is very good to be set in an azure ring. Also Isidore says that this magnet is a stone of India, coloured somewhat like iron; and it is found in India among the troglodytes, and draws iron to himself; and it is found in India, so that it makes as it were a chain of iron with rings, as Isidore says; therefore in the common speech this stone is called 'quick iron'. The strength and the virtue of it is so great, as Augustine says, that even if a stone is set under a vessel of gold or of brass and iron is set on it, by the moving of the stone that is beneath the iron set above it will move. Also it is said that there is in another country in a temple an image of iron, and it seems that the image hangs in the air. And in Ethiopia is another kind of magnet that forsakes iron and drives it away from itself. Also the magnet draws iron into a corner, and the bluer he is the better he is. Also Dioscorides and the lapidary say that this stone reconciles and brings into accord love between men and their wives. Also it gives grace and fairness in speech and in word. Also in a drink made of honey and wine it helps the dropsy and the spleen and the falling evil, and also for burning. Platearius says that witches use this stone very much.

---

[111] Evans and Serjeantson read (incorrectly) 'Iudea'.

drye in þe dryþ[112] þegre. And þer ben moyntens in þe see of schilce magnes, & þerfor þey drawen to him & brekyne schippis þat ben Inayled with yerne. Also þe powder of audamant, put it into a woynde, it draweþ owte yerne of þe wounde. Also auycen seyþe þat ~~luys of fenel is g~~ þe pouder of þe adamant, þe quantyte of ij drammes, with þe Iues of fenel, is gode for þe dropsy & aȝens þe splene & for fallyng of heere.

Also this stone magnet is dry in the third degree. And there are mountains of magnet in the sea of Cilicia, and therefore they draw towards them and break ships that are nailed with iron. Also with the powder of diamond, put it into a wound, and it draws iron out of the wound. Also Avicenna says that the powder of the diamond, the quantity of two drams, with juice of fennel, is good for the dropsy and against the spleen and for hair loss.

108. [Sapphire]

Saphyr is a ston ryȝt comly one a ryng vpone a kyngis fynger; & god haue ȝeve to him myche grace. Men taken him ~~aȝen~~ in general[114] lymbe in a flod of þe eest besydes a roche of þe see, & þat þey ben so fonde. Some ben mor gentill þen oþer; þo þat ben most gentill of color & most lyke Inde, þey semble to þe clen color of heuen; & in þe dep waters ben founde saphirs þat ben derke, & þey ben ful of vertues & better, þe[n] clene oþer maner saphirs þat ben lasse worþe, & þey ben vertues & full of grace. Þese iij maners of saphirs distrowen fowlnes & envy, & comforteþ þe body & membres, & letteþ þe man fro enprisonyng; & he þat with þe saphir towcheþ þe iiij places of þe

Sapphire is a stone that is very beautiful on a ring on a king's finger, and God has given him much grace. Men take him in general from a branch of a river of the east beside a rock of the sea, and they are found in this manner. Some are more gentle than others, and those that are more gentle in colour and most like India resemble the pure colour of heaven; and in the deep waters are found sapphires that are dark, and they are full of virtues and better than the other pure kind of sapphires that are of less value, and they are virtuous and full of grace. These three kinds of sapphires destroy foulness and envy, and comfort the body and limbs, and release a man from

---

[112] Evans and Serjeantson read '[þ]ry[d]'.

[114] Evans and Serjeantson suggest this may be a scribal error for 'in grauel of'.

prison of of þe cheynes, if he haue gode beleue he schal be delyuerd by vertu of þe ston þat god haþe gyfe to þe saphire & granted. The bok tellen vs þat þe saphir is wel good to acord men togidder, & to brek wychecraft; & it is mych worþe to hele byles & swellyng; if it be geven to him þat haþe byles or swellyng with-in þe body, anon he schall be hole by vertu þat gode haþe gyuen þerto; and it schall kele[115] þe body of hot syknes, & do awaye þe sorowȝ of þe hede, & it helpeþ þe seknes of goomes, & chaseþ owte þe ange of yene. And þe boke seyþe þat gode counseyleþe him to ber it clenly, for it makeþ a man to haue wyte & myȝt; þey schuld leve a clen lyfe þat beren þis vertues stone. Þe boke telleþ vs þat þe saphir is of þe color of hevene. Also sente Iohn seyþe in þe apocalyps þe saphir was þe secund fundament in þe heuenly ierusalem. Also þe saphir schold be wassh in mylke & Indronke, & for all yuellis in a mannes body, & for ache of þe hede & for þe palesye. Þe best saphirs ben þoo þat ben in þe este or in ynde, & namly if it haþe as it were powder of gold ymedeld þeryn. Þis saphir stone is þyke & not passyng bryȝt, as Ised seyþe. Þis ston is most Iprysed in þe lapidary; & for he is so noble & so excellent, þerfor he is clepid gemma gemmarum, as wer chef of precios stones, for

imprisonment, and he who touches four places of the prison of his chains with a sapphire, if he has good belief, will be delivered by virtue of the stone that God has given and granted to the sapphire. The book tells us that the sapphire is very good to bring men together, and to break witchcraft; and it is of great worth to heal boils and swelling within the body; soon he will be whole by the virtue that God has given it, and it will heal the body of hot sickness, and do away headache, and it helps sickness of the gums, and chases out soreness of the eyes. And the book says that God counsels him to bear it in purity, for it makes a man have understanding and strength; they should live a pure life who bear this virtuous stone. The book tells us that the sapphire is of the colour of heaven. Also St John says in the Apocalypse that the sapphire was the second foundation in the heavenly Jerusalem. Also the sapphire should be washed in milk and the milk drunk for all evils in a man's body, and for headache and for the palsy. The best sapphires are those that are in the east or in India, and especially if it has (as it were) powder of gold mixed in it. This sapphire stone is thick and not especially bright, as Isidore says. This stone is most prized in the lapidary, since he is so noble and so excellent, and

---

[115] Read 'hele'?

65

kepeþ þe body & saveþ [fol. 12v] þe lymes hole & sounde; & he haþe a bryȝt ster, by þe bryȝtnes of þat sterre & þerby his vertu is knowen Also þer is anoder maner of saphir which is cleped sirtices, & he is founde fast by þat plasis þat is cleped cirtes, amonge þe grauell of þe see libicum. Also dias seyþ þat he is founde in þe veynes of vermylon, þis laȝurine is founde; also þe sam vaynes of saphir in in þe myddell & as it wer in þe wombe is a certen kynde of carbuccle yfounde; þerfor many men suppose þat þe saphir is carbuccles moder; for many men seyn þat þe carbuccle is gendyr in þe saphir veynes; & many men seyn þat þe carbuccle is sodenle beschawed[116] wiþ a certen blew lyke of þe kynde of saphir, as dias seyþe. Also he haþe vertu to confort & to glade þe hert þerfor. It is seyd þat he helpeþ aȝens þe cardeacle & aȝens al malyncoly passiouns; þerfor it stancheþ rennyng & swetyng that comeþ to swyþe. Also dias seyþe þe same; ande he haþe vertu to stanche blode; & so þe saphir of þe eest stancheþ bledyng at þe nose if it is leyd to þe temples. Also he haþe a syngler vertu þat þe saphir abateþ bolnynges & swellynges of postomes þat is clepid antrax, for he putteþ þe myȝt of ventosite & þe malice of þe postom, for he ouercomeþ & putteþ owte þe wodnes þerof, & suffereþ not þe

therefore he is called 'gem of gems', as it were chief of precious stones, for he keeps the body and preserves the limbs whole and sound. And he has a bright star; by the brightness of that star his virtue is known. Also there is another kind of sapphires which is called *syrticis*, and he is found close by that place which is called Syrtis, in the gravel of the Libyan sea. Also Dioscorides says that he is found in the veins of vermillion, where this lazurine is found; also the same veins of sapphire are found in the middle and (as it were) in the womb of a certain kind of carbuncle; therefore many men suppose that the sapphire is carbuncle's mother; for many men say that the carbuncle is born in the sapphire's veins; and many men say that the carbuncle is suddenly overshadowed with a certain blue like that of sapphire, as Dioscorides says. Also he has the virtue to comfort and gladden the heart. It is said that he helps against cardiac and against all melancholy passions; therefore it staunches bloody flux and sweating that comes too swiftly. Also Dioscorides says the same; and he has the virtue of staunching blood; and so the sapphire of the east staunches nosebleeds if it is laid against the temples. Also he has a singular virtue: the sapphire reduces swellings and impostumes that are

---

[116] Evans and Serjeantson suggest the reading 'beschadewed'.

smeke þerof to come to þe hert; for his malice infecteþ þe spirites. Also his vertu is contrary to venym, & he qwencheþ it euery dele. And so yf þu wilt preve it, [put] an attorcope in a box, & hal a very saphir of ynde at þe mowþe a while, & by vertu þerof he is ouercome & dyeþ as it wer sodenly, as dias seyþ, & þe sam I haue assayd oftyn in many diuers places. Also his vertu kepeþ & saveþ þe syȝt & clenseþ þe yene of fylþe withowte eny greuance. Þerfor it is wryten in bokes þat it takeþ away þe ache of þe forhede. Also þis ston was of gret autorite in old tyme, þat men seyd þat þey wold holowȝ it to hir god, & so it was syngulerly holowed to her god appolyne. For when naciouns axedet consel of appolyn in tyme of sacrifice, þey hope to be certefy & to haue answer þe raþer if saf saphir ston wer present as Dias seyþe. And þer is þe soþe þat þey þat vsen nygramancie seyn þat þe mowene haue answer of god & more Iherd by þe saphir þen be oþer precios stones. And also wycches louen syngulerly wel þis stone, for þey byleuen þat þey done certeyn wonders by þe vertu of þis ston. Also þis ston doþe away sorrow and dred, & putteþ fere, & makeþ a man bold & hardy & mayster & wictor; and it makeþ þe hert stedfast in godnes, & it makeþ a man meke & myld & godly. Et qui portat eum castissimus esse iubetur.

called anthrax, for he puts away the strength of flatulence and the malice of the impostume, for he overcomes and removes the smart of it, and does not allow the pain of it to cause hurt to you; for his malice infects the spirits. Also his virtue is contrary to venom, and he quenches it every time. And so if you want to prove it, put a spider in a box, and hold a true sapphire of India at the mouth for a while, and by the virtue of it he is overcome and dies suddenly, as Dioscorides says, and the same I have tried often in many different places. Also this virtue keeps and preserves the sight and cleanses the eyes from impurities without any pain. Therefore it is written in books that it takes away the ache of the forehead. Also this stone was of great authority in ancient times, so that men said that they would consecrate it to their god, and so it was particularly sacred to their god Apollo. For when nations asked counsel of Apollo at the time of sacrifice, they hoped to be certain and have an answer if a sapphire stone was present, as Dioscorides says. And there is the truth that those who use necromancy say that they are more able to have answer of God and are more heard by the sapphire than by other precious stones. And also witches love this stone especially well, for they believe that they do certain wonders by the virtue of this stone. Also this stone does away sorrow and dread, and puts away fear, and makes a man bold and hardy and master and victor; and it makes the heart steadfast in goodness, and it makes a man meek and mild and godly. And he who bears it is commanded to be most chaste.

109. [Emerald]

Smaradd*us* is a ston most p*r*ecios of al gren*e* stones, as Ised seyþe. Men i*n* þe old tyme ȝaue þerto þe þryd dignyte aft*er* margarites. And smaragd*us* haþe þe name aboue al p*r*ecios stones of gre*n* colo*r*s. For it is seyd þ*at* all gren erbis & all gre*n* stones þ*at* ben p*r*ecios ben not so g[r]en i*n* colo*r* as is þis ston smaragd*us*, for it passeþ i*n* gren*n*es erbes and grase & twygges or sprotte for he enfecteþ þe eyr abowte hi*m* wi*th* his passyng gre*n* colo*r*, as Ised seyþ; & his color abateþ not i*n* þe sone i*n* no man*er* wyse. No þy*n*g co*m*forteþ **[fol. 13r]** þe eyene þat greue mor þen þis ston; for if þe body þerof is cle*n*sed, þen ymage be*n* þerin as it wer a mirror. For þe Emperor Cesare*us* vsed to see Fyȝti*n*g of swerd-men i*n* þis ston, as Ised seyþ. And þerof ben xij man*er* of kyndes, þ*at* þe most noble ben yfou*n*de i*n* acia, þ*at* is in ge*n*te scitica, & bredam holdeþ þe second p\e/lase. And smaragd*us* ben fonde vndir ston*n*es & i*n* chynnes þerof when þe norþe*n* wynde bloweþ, for þe erþe is vnhilled & þe stones

Emerald is the most precious of all green stones, as Isidore says. Men in ancient times gave it the third dignity after pearls. And emerald has a name above all other stones of green colour. For it is said that all green herbs and all green stones that are precious are not as green in colour as this stone emerald, for it surpasses in green-ness herbs and grass and twigs or sprouts, for he infects the atmosphere around him with his surpassing green colour, as Isidore says; and his colour does not diminish in the sun in any way. Nothing comforts eyes that grieve more than this stone; for if the body of it is cleaned, then the image therein is as it were a mirror. For the Emperor Caesar used to see the fighting of swordsmen in this stone, as Isidore says. And there are twelve kinds of it, the most noble of which are found in Asia, that is, amongst the Scythian people, and [*meaning uncertain*] holds the second place. And emerald is found under stones and in their chines when the northern wind smaragd*us* schine*n* amo*n*ge þe stones, for in southe wynd gr*a*uel & sonde be most Imoved. Þe egipcions han þe iij smaragd*us*, & þey ben fonde in metel or in*e* ore of brase, but þey gleymy*n*g for þey haue spekes lyke vnto brase or to lede or to salte. Þow3 þe smaragd*us* be*n* grene by kende, 3it þer ben oþer smaragd*us* þat gone owte of kynde, for þey ben vnworchiped by veynes of brase & þe[y] ben called calce smaragd*us*. All þes seyþ Ised. And þ*is* ston is Itak & beneme fro gryfes; and plente of smaragd*us* may not be fonde, for gret grifes letten þe comyng of men be þe wey þat ledeþ þerto, as Ised seyþ. Also þ*is* ston multeplyeþ his grene color; of hi*m* comeþ a beme þat þeyþ þe eyre abowte hi*m* & makeþ hi*m* grene. Þe body þerof is cler & of mirror kynde, & scheweþ fig*u*res, ymag*es* & schappis of þy*n*ges þat ben mor ny3 þerto; and it haþe a 3ifte of kynde, a benefite of vertu, to saue & hell dyu*er*se syk*n*es & yuell. Also dias seyþ he increseþ riches, & makeþ me*n* to haue goode wordes & feyr*e*, & euyde*n*ce of & cause of plee. If þ*is* ston is hanged abowte þe neke, it helpeþ emitritene & þe fally*n*g yuel, & saueþ & co*m*forteþ febell sy3t; & he chasteþ lecheres meuy*n*ges, & makeþ gode mend; & it helpeþ a3e*ns* al fanta3ies & iapes of fendes, & ceseþ tempest & stancheþ blod. And it is seyd þat it helpeþ hem þat vsen to dyuyne &

blows, for the earth is flat and emerald shines among the stones, for in the south wind gravel and sand must be moved. The Egyptians have three emeralds, and they are found in metal or in ore of brass, but they gleam for they have specks like brass or lead or salt. Although the emerald is green by nature, yet there are other emeralds that depart from nature, for they are not honoured by veins of brass and they are called calce emeralds. All this Isidore says. And this stone is taken and stolen from griffins; and plenty of emeralds may not be found, for great griffins hinder the coming of men by the way that leads to them, as Isidore says. Also this stone multiplies his green colour; from him comes a beam that dyes the air around him and makes him green. The body of it is clear and of the nature of a mirror, and reveals figures, images and shapes of things that are near to it; and it has a gift of nature, a benefit of virtue, to save and heal many sicknesses and evils. Also Dioscorides says he increases riches, and makes men have good and fair words, and evidence of and cause of plea. If this stone is hung around the neck it helps intermittent fever and the falling evil, and saves and comforts feeble sight; and he chastens lecherous tendencies, and makes good mind; and it helps against all fantasies and japes of fiends, and stops tempests and gessen what schall fall, at[117] it is seyd *in* bok*es*. Also whoso bere*þ* *þis* stone smaragd*us in* clene lyfe, his sy3t schal neu*er* fayl hi*m*, & his colo*ur* schal eu*er* be fayer, & he schal be loued of all men & wome*n*, ne he schal neu*er* be trayed, ne neu*er* lese his gode, but eu*er* encrese i*n* riches & loue, & it kepe*þ* fro al myshappis & disestes.

staunches blood. And it is said that it helps them who are accustomed to divine and guess what will befall, as it is said in books. Also whoever bears this stone emerald in a pure life, his sight will never fail him, and his colour will ever be fair, and he will be loved by all men and women, nor will he ever lose his goods, but always increase in riches and love, and it preserves from all mishaps and disasters.

110. [Sardine]

Sardis is a p*r*ecious stone, & he is of a red colo*ur*, as it were red er*þe*; & he he he ha*þe þe* name for he was first fou*n*de *in* sardis, as Ised sey*þ*. For, a*s þe* glose vpo*n*e *þe* apocalips sey*þe*, *þ*ow3 *þis* stone be p*r*eciose & fayre, 3it many me*n* cou*n*te hi*m* lest wor*þe* amo*n*ge p*r*eciose stones; for as *þ*ey sey, owte take schyny*n*g *þ*er is no p*r*ofite *þ*er*with* but *þ*at only *þ*e sto*n*e onix may not greue in his p*r*esenss; for as it is seyd, *þ*at *þis* ston onichul ha*þe* some yuel p*r*op*ir*tes, & he may not schew he*m* yn dede i*n þe* p*r*esens of *þis* sto*n*e sard*us*. And dias sey*þe þ*at ou*er þis* ve*r*tu sard*us* ha*þe* many od*er* ve*r*tues. Of sardi*us þ*er ben x man*er* of kyndes, but *þ*e best come*þ* owte of sardi*us*; & he is gode for [*illeg.*] for encrese*þ* ioye & putte*þ* away dredl & he make*þ* a ma*n*e bold & hardy, & he

Sardine is a precious stone, and he is of a red colour, like red earth. And he has that name because he was first found in Sardis, as Isidore says. For as the Gloss on the Apocalypse says, although this stone is precious and fair, yet many men consider him less valuable among precious stones, for they say that apart from shining there is no profit in it, apart from that the stone onyx may not cause harm in his presence. For it is said that this stone onyx has some evil properties, and he may not show them at all in the presence of this stone sardine. And Dioscorides says that aside from this virtue sardine has many other virtues. There are ten kinds of sardine; and he is good for [*illeg.*], for increasing joy and putting away dread, and he makes a man bold

---

[117] Evans and Serjeantson read 'a[s]'.

70

schappeþ þe wyle. And þe ston onyx may not grefe *in* his *pr*esens. Also he seyþe þ*at* sardo*us* þ*at* is all red kepeþ his berer fro enchantheme*ntes* & fro wyche-crafte. Also þe lapidarie seyþ þ*at* sardi*us* & grenas & alama*n*di*n*es & iagu*n*ces ben wexy*n*g togiders; but þe iagu*n*ce haþe þe ve*r*tu of al þese stones, & it is þe most fine þyng of þe verld, for his colo*ur* is gentil & red; & it makeþ a ma*n* glad & to dwele *in* ʒonge & trewþe; & he makeþ a man to forʒete his cont*r*ariosite & his bey*n*g; and dowʒt þe nowʒt as of no sty*n*g worme n*e* wild best. Also me*n* may passen perlose wat*er* mych þe raþ*er*. And whoso haþe it vpon*e* his fynggere, mych þe leu*er* he schall recyue geest*es* to herbarowʒ; [fol. 13v] and when he schaweþ þe iagu*n*ce ston, of þ*at* he preye to men reasonably it schal not be hid fro hi*m*. Also þe boke telleþ vs þ*at* god named fyrst þ*is* stone, & was of color of þe erþe, of red erþe wherof god made fyrst ma*n*, adam, *in* þe feld of Damaske, wherof we be of þe self behetyng, & þ*er*for named god þ*is* ston first, & *in* þ*at* it is of þe self color. Sent Iohn seyþe *in* þe apocalyps þ*at* he saue þ*is* ston in þe vj fondame*n*t of þe very kyngdome.

and hardy, and he forms the will. And the stone onyx may not cause harm in his presence. Also he says that the sardine that is completely red preserves his bearer from enchantments and from witch-craft. Also the lapidary says that sardines and garnets and and alemandines and jacinths grow together; but jacinth has the virtue of all of these stones, and it is the most fine thing in the world, for his colour is gentle and red, and it makes a man glad and helps him stay young and true; and he makes a man forget his enmity and his status; and you have no need to fear any stinging insect or wild beast. Also men may pass over dangerous water much better. And whoever has it on his finger, he will much easier receive guests to host; and when he shows the jacinth stone, whatever he asks reasonably of men will not be withheld from him. Also the book tells us that God named this stone first, and it was the colour of the earth, of the red earth from which God made the first man, Adam, in the field of Damascus, of which we are of the same descent; and therefore God named this stone first, and because it is of the same colour. St John says in the Apocalypse that he saw this stone in the sixth foundation of the very kingdom.

111. [Sardonyx]

Sardonix. Þis stone haþe þe name of ij stones of sardius & onix, as Ised seyþ; & he is of iij colors; for þe blak is of þe lowest, & þe whitʒ of þe medel, þe rede as vermylon is hiest. Only þis ston takeþ not only of þe wax when he is þer-in. And it is fonde in araby & in ynde. & þerof ben v maners of kynde, but which hym haþe moste many colours, & most distingned, & is most pyche, he is best. It is seyd þat he putteþ awaye lechery, & makeþ a man mek & chast. Þe lapidarie seyþe þat þis ston sardonix is a ston redissh reednes & blakkyssh. Þis ston by himself adaunteþ wreþe of a man & makeþ him rest wel by nyʒt withowte myche dremyng or noyng taches, & it doþe awaye noyng vices fro men & kepeþ him chast & schamefast & graciose.

Sardonyx. The stone has the name of the two stones, sardius and onyx, as Isidore says; and he is of two colours. For the black is the lowest, and the white in the middle, and the red like vermillion is the highest [in value]. Only this stone does not take only of the wax when he is in it. And it is found in Arabia and in India. And there are five kinds of it, but the one who has the most colours, and is most distinguished, and is most pointed is the best. It is said that he puts away lechery, and makes a man meek and chaste. The lapidary says that this stone sardonyx is reddish and blackish stone. This stone by himself subdues the wrath of a man and makes him rest well by night without much dreaming or annoying blemishes, and it removes annoying vices from men and and keeps them chaste and modest and gracious.

112. [Serpentine]

Serpentyne is a stone of dyuerse colours, & it comeþ owte of perce, & it is red, blak & grene; for þe panter is of diuers colours þerfor þis stone haþe þe name of panter, for al maner beestes maken myche of þe best because of his bewete & of his coloures and his swet smel. And he þat bereþ þis ston vpone him he is gladly kept fro all yuelles; and

Serpentine is a stone of different colours, and it comes out of Persia, and is red, black and green; for the panther is of different colours, therefore this stone has the name panther, for all kinds of beasts make much of the beast because of his beauty and his colours and his sweet smell. And he who bears this stone on him is gladly preserved from all also he is gode for venym.

evils; and also he is good for venom.

113. [Topaz]

Topaces is a stone þat haþe a ȝelowe color, and þer ben moo þen oone maner, þat one of þe eest; and owte of araby comeþ þe best. Topaces makeþ cold a malady þat is cleped þe feyr; and þe feyr þat is quenched wiþ topace schal neuer wax after. Þe boke seyþe þe topace draweþ him to semblence of þe mone which is fowle & reyne, þen þis ston is more fowle; and when þe ȝonge mone is most fayr, þen it is mor fayr of color & gentil. He þat bereþ þis ston schall loue to lede his body chastly, & þen mor to loke heuenly wayes. Þe bible seyþ þis ston was þe ij stone vp vpone þe brest of aarone, þe which haþe þe color of gold. Sent Iohn seyþe in þe apocolyps þat he say þis stone in þe ix fundement of þe [e]uerlastyng cite. By þe morn kynges sholden bleþly beholdene topace, for he gefeþ hem gode remembrance to loke to þe rial ~~lyk~~ lyf þat he schal haue, which is chowned[118] in heuen, þat schal neuer fayl. Also þo þat beholden many stones in sobernes tornen mor her syȝt to þe topacie. Holy writ seyþe þat þe topace such as he vaxeþ is best; but it is not so pleyn ne no hete may be pulisched of him, þerfor he leseþ not his ~~syȝt~~

Topaz is a stone that has a yellow colour, and there is more than one kind; one from the east, and out of Arabia comes the best. Topazes cool a malady which is called 'the fire'; and the fire that is quenched with topaz will never ignite afterwards. The book says that the topaz corresponds to the moon, and when it is foul and wet, then this stone is more foul. And when the young moon is more fair, then it is more fair and gentle in colour. He who bears this stone will love to lead his body chastly, and then to look more to heavenly ways. The Bible says this stone was the second stone on the breast of Aaron, which had the colour of gold. St John says in the Apocalypse that he saw this stone in the ninth foundation of the everlasting city. In the morning kings should blithely look on topaz, for he gives them good remembrance to look to the royal life they should have, which is crowned in heaven, and which will never fail. Also, those who look on many stones in sobriety turn their sight more to topaz. Holy writ says that the topaz who grows is best, but it is not so plain that no heat may be polished from him, therefore he does not lose his

---

[118] Evans and Serjeantson read 'c[r]owned'.

strengþe. Also þis topacie comeþ owte of a flode of þe eest orient, and of þes þer ben ij maners, but þat oone is mor cler þen þe oder. And eche þe mone is cler, þe ston is cler, and when þe mone is troble þe ston is troble; & he schal be set in gold. Also Ised seyþe þat þis ston is a schyny[n]g kynge & with al colowurs schyneþ; & it was forst Ifonde in a yel of arabie, in þe whiche yle-londe þe trogadite wer disesed with honger & tempest; & þey dyggen vp rotes of herbis, & þer þey founde þis ston þer-with, & þey clepid it testamnebulis; þerafter schipmen souȝten & founde it, & clepid it topazim in þe langga[g]e of þe trogadites; þerfor þis ston þat was so y-sowȝt & founde is cleped \a/ topazius, and it haþe name of þe londe of topazim in her langgage, & it & it is seyngische; & it is þe most grete of precios strones. Plinius wrote þat a [fol. 14r] ston of þis kynde was yfonde so grete & so myche þat philade[l]phe made an ymage þer-of, iiij cubites of lengþe. Also in þe glose vpone þe apocalyps it is seyþ in þis maner; þe more scarse þis topazius is, þe mor preciose he is; and he haþe ij colors as it were of gold & clere eyre. And he schyneþ most when he is smeten with þe soone-beme, and passeþ in clernes al oþer stones þat ben precios; & he comforteþ men & beestes to behold & þer to loke þer-vpone. And if þu wypest þis ston he wole be more derk, & if þu love him in

strength. Also this topaz comes from a river of the far east, and there are two kinds of them, but one is clearer than the other. And when the moon is clear, the stone is clear, and when the moon is cloudy, the stone is cloudy; and he should be set in gold. Also Isidore says that this stone is a shining king and shines with all colours. And it was first found in an island of Arabia, in which land the troglodytes were troubled with famine and tempest; and they were digging up roots of herbs, and there they found this stone with them, and they called it *testamnebulis*; thereafter seamen sought and found it, and called it topaz in the language of the troglodytes. Therefore this stone that was sought and found in this way is called a topaz, and it has the name of the land of Topazim in their language. And it is most transparent, and it is the greatest of precious stones. Pliny wrote that a stone of this kind was so found so great and so large that Philadelphus made an image out of it, of four cubits in length. Also in the Gloss on the Apocalypse it is said in this way: the more scarce topaz is, the more precious he is; and he has two colours, as it were of gold and a clear day. And he shines most when he is struck by a sunbeam, and surpasses in transparency all other stones that are precious; and he comforts men and beasts to look upon him. And if you wipe this stone he will be his owen kend he wol be mor cler; and in the tresor of kyngges no þyng is mor cler nor mor preciose þen þis preciose ston is; for clernes of himself he takeþ to him þe clernes of all oþer preciose stones þat ben abowte him. And it is seyd þat he foloweþ þe course of þe mone, & þerfor he helpeþ aȝens þe passioun of lynatik folke; and so it seyd in þe lapidairy, þat as þe mone is more ful or lasse so effecte is mor of þis ston or lesse. Also he stancheþ blode, & he helpeþ hem þat han þe emoroides & swageþ him. And he wold not suffre feruent water for to boile, as it is seyd in bokes. Dias seyþe þat it asswageþ boþe wraþ & sorowȝ, & it helpeþ aȝens yuel þowȝtes & frenesy, & aȝens soden deþe. And he haþe þe schap of a mirror; and þe ymage þat is þeryne is seene in a holowȝ mirror. Also, if þu preve þis ston, put him in a hote water þat is boylyng, & if he lese his colour þen he is nowȝt.

darker, and if you love him in his own way he will be more transparent; and in the treasury of kings nothing is clearer or more precious than this precious stone; for he takes to himself the transparency of all other precious stones that are around him. And it is said that he follows the course of the moon, and therefore he helps against the suffering of lunatics; and so it says in the lapidary, that when the moon is more full or less, so the effect on this stone is more or less. Also he staunches blood, and he helps those who have haemorrhoids and assuages them. And he will not allow bubbling water to boil, as it is said in books. Dioscorides says that it assuages both wrath and sorrow, and it helps against evil thoughts and frenzy, and against sudden death. And he has the form of a mirror, and the image that is within is seen in a hollow mirror. Also, if you [want to] prove this stone, put him in hot water that is boiling, and if he loses his colour then he is of no value.

114. [Pearl]

Margarita is chef of al stons þat ben wyȝt & preciose, as Ised seyþ. And it haþe þe name margarita for it is founde in shellis which ben cokelis or in mosclys & in schellfyssh of þe see; þis bredyng is schellfyssh, & it is genderd of þe dewe of heuen, which dewe þe

Pearl is the chief of all stones that are white and precious, as Isidore says. And it has the name *margarita* because it is found in cockleshells or in mussels and in shellfish of the sea; this growth in shellfish comes about from the dew of heaven; the shellfish schell fish receyueþ in certen tymes of þe ȝer, of þe which dew margarites comen. Some ben cleped vnyons, & þey han a conable name, for þer is oonly one Ifonde & neuer ij togeder; and þe whiȝt margarites ben better þen þe ȝelow, & þo þat ben conceyued of þe morrow dew ben made dym with þe eyr of euentyde: hucusque Isodorus. Also some ben fonde which ben perced kenly, & þe[y] ben better þen þat oþer; and some ben persed by crafte, as Plato seyþ. And þey ben best wyȝt, cler & rownde; & þey han vertu of comfort by al kend þerof; and somme seyne þat þey comforten lymes & membris, for it clenseþ him of superfluite of humours & fasten þe lymes, & helpen aȝen þe cordiacle passioun & aȝens swonyng of hert, & aȝens febilnes of Flux by cause of medecyne, & Also aȝens rennyng of blod, & aȝens þe flyx of þe wombe, as plato seyþ. Also in plato it is seyd þat margarites ben gendred of þe morow dewe, & some mor & some lesse, but it is trowed þat no margarite groweþ past halfe a fote. Also it is seyd þat when lyȝtnynge or þundrige falleþ, when þe margarite schold bred of þe dew þat it resseyueþ, þe schel closeþ be most soden strengeþ & þe gendringes faileþ & is cast owte. Þe best & most [n]oblyst margarites comen owt of ynde & of old brytayn.

receives this dew at certain times of the year, from which pearls comes. Some are called unions, and they have a memorable name, for only one is ever found and never two together. And white pearls are better than yellow ones, and those that were conceived from the morning dew are made dim with the air of eventide (as we find in Isidore). Also some are found which are sharply pierced, and they are better than the other; and some are pierced by art, as Plato says. And they are best when white, clear and round; and all kinds of them have the virtue of comfort; and some say that they comfort limbs and members, for they cleanse them of superfluity of humours and make the limbs fast, and help against cardiac passion and against swooning of heart, and against feebleness of bloody flux caused by medicine, and also against running of blood, and against the flux of the womb, as Plato says. Also in Plato it is said that pearls are born of the morning dew, and some are greater and some are smaller, but it is sure that no pearl grows beyond half a foot. Also it is said that when lightning or thunder falls, at the time when the pearl should grow from the dew that it receives, he will close with very sudden strength and the beginnings fail and are cast out. The best and most noble pearls come out of India and from Great Britain.

115. [Medus]

Medus is a precios ston, & is fonde in þe lond of medeis, and it is sumtyme grene & sumtime blak, as Diascorides seyþe. And som sey þat he is founde in þe sowþe londe. Þis ston ȝeueþ boþe deþe & lyfe. Þe vertu of þis stone is aȝenst blynndnes of yȝene, & aȝens potagre, if it be temperd with þe mylk of a woman þat norschiþ a man child. Also it is gode for ache of þe reynes & ek for þe frenesey; & if þe blak stone be leyd in water, & lete dri[n]ke þe water, it distroyeþ sp[e]wyng & ouer-comyng of þe stomak; & if þe forhed eider þe yene be wasshin þer [fol. 14v] with, it distroyeþ wonderly þe webbe þat greueþ þe syȝt; & if he drynk þis licor he schal be dede. Þis ston is blak, but his vertues ben whiȝte when þey helpen & blak whene þey noyene. Som men seyn þat þe mylk beforseyd schold be gode for yene þat ben blynd. And who dis-tempereþ it with þe mylk of a schepe þat haþe not had but oone lambe, & it be a male, it schal helpe þe potagre & þe syknes of oþer lymes; & it will be tempered in siluer, & when it is temperid þen [ȝ]if it to þe seke bodi with wyne; and when he is distempered with water he haþe ale his kynde; and afterward it schal be ȝeuen to Wassh with yene, & þey schol be

Medus is a precious stone, and is found in the land of the Medes, and it is sometimes green and sometimes black, as Dioscorides says. And some say that he is found in the southern land. This stone gives both death and life. The virtue of this stone is against blindness of the eyes, and against gout, if it is mixed with the milk of woman who nourishes a boy child. Also it is good for ache of the kidneys and even for the frenzy. And if the black stone is laid in water, and someone drinks the water, it takes away vomiting and overturning of the stomach; and if either the forehead or the eyes are washed with it, it wondrously destroys the web that grieves the sight;[119] and if he drinks this liquid he will be dead. This stone is black, but his virtues are white when they help and black when they hurt. Some men say that the aforesaid milk should be good for eyes that are blind. And whoever mixes it with the milk of a sheep that has had only one lamb, which is male, it will help the gout and the sickness of other limbs; and it will be mixed with silver; and when it is mixed then give it to the sick person with wine; and when he is mixed with water he has all his nature; and afterwards it should be given to

---

[119] Cataracts.

77

hole.

wash the eyes, and they will be whole.

116. [Onyx]

Onychinus is a stone of ynde & of arabie. He haþe in himself color ymedeled lyke þe mayle of onix. Þe onix of yie[120] haþe colour of fyre with whiȝt veynes & strakes, and þe ston onix of arabie haþe blak vaynes. And þer [ben] v maner of kyndes; oone is sardonix, & he haþe þat name of cumpanye of tweyne, of þe which stones of þe onix & rednes of þe sardius, as it is seyd ynnermor in þe sardonice. Also it is seyd þat þis ston onix haþe many noyful effectes, as dias seyþe, for if it is borne abowte þe neke eyþer fynger, he exciteþ sorowȝ & elyngnese & dred, & it multeplyeþ plee, & ȝeueþ þe hert to contencioun & strife, & exciteþ in childre noyful superfluyte of spetel; and it may not noye neiþer greue in þe precens of þe stone sardius. Þis stone onix is cler & of þe kynd of mirroures, þerfor ymages & schappis ben yseyne þeryne as it wer in a mirror, but þat is dyuersely & derkely, as dias seyþe.

Onyx is a stone from India and from Arabia. He has in himself a colour mixed like the male onyx. The onyx of India has the colour of fire with white veins and streaks, and the onyx of Arabia has black veins. And there are five kinds: one is sardonyx, and he has that name from the joining of two, the onyx and the redness of sardine, as is said under the sardonyx. Also it is said that this stone onyx has many harmful effects, as Dioscorides says, for if it is borne around the neck or finger, he excites sorrow and melancholy and dread, and it multiplies pleas, and gives the heart over to contention and strife, and excites in children an annoying excess of saliva; and it may neither annoy nor grieve in the presence of the stone sardine. This stone onyx is transparent and of the nature of mirrors; therefore images and shapes are seen in it just as in a mirror, but scattered and darkly, as Dioscorides says.

117. [Obsidian]

Obxianus is a stone þat if a man ber him þer schall neuer sweueness to him harme, ne no man

Obsidian is a stone that if a man bears him, dream visions will never do him harm, nor will any

---

[120] Evans and Serjeantson read 'y[nd]e'.

schall spek him harme, so þat þe ston shyne vpone him. Also ber it vpone þe and þow schalt neuer have yuel deþe.

man speak harm to him, as long as the stone shines on him. Also bear it upon you and you will never have an evil death.

118. [Oblyx]

Oblyx is a stone & is lik to horn of a mannis nayle, & mydes as it were colour of whiȝt. Whoso bereþ þis stone schal be de fyrst þat schal be scomfite in batayle.

Oblyx is a stone that is like a man's nail, and in the middle is like the colour of white. Whoever bears this stone will be the first who will be discomforted in battle.

119. [Enisus]

Enysus is a stone, who þat bereþ it schall neuer have rest in his slepe. No noþer vertu know I in him. To preue him, frote him on þy tonge, & þy mowþe schal be blak.

Enisus is a stone, and whoever bears it will never have rest in his sleep. I know no other virtue in him. To prove him, rub him on your tongue, and your mouth will be black.

120. [Melichros]

Melotes is a stone, & it haþe þat name for swetnes þat comeþ owte þerof, as wer hony, as Ised seyþ; & it haþe ij colours, it is lyk gren on þat oone syde, & lyke hony one þat oþer syde.

Melichros is a stone that is renowned for the sweetness that comes out of it, like honey, as Isidore says; and it has two colours: it is like green on one side, and like honey on the other side.

121. [Myrrhite]

Merites is a preciose stone, & it haþe þat name for it is lyk to myrre color; & if it is wronge or pressed it smelleþ swete as narde.

Myrrhite is a precious stone, and it has that name because it is similar to myrrh in colour, and if it is wrung or pressed it smells as sweet as nard.

122. [Ruby]

Rubie is a red stone shynyng, & he strengþiþ al stones þat ben rede, as þe boke telleþ. Þe gentel rubie þat is fyne & clene is lord of al stones, & he is also as water of wateris. It haþe vertu above all oþer precios stones, & he is of shuch lordschip þat when he þat comeþ bereþ it amonge oþer men, all þey schul do him honor & grace, & al men mak ioye of his comynge. Þe boke telleþ vs þat þe beestes þat drinke of þe water wher þe rubie haþe be wete yne schul be hole of her siknes; & he þat haþe discomfort in goddis beleve, & behold þis stone, it schall comforte him & make him to forȝete his contrariosite bl vertu þat god haþe ȝeuen þerto. It fedeþ a man & comforteþ his hert & his body, & it wynneþ a man lord-ship. Þer ben iij gret rubies, & ben fonde in þe londe of libie in a flod of paradise. Moyses put þis stone in þe brest of aarone in þe ij corner of þe xij stones. Also þis stone clenseþ yene & comforteþ þe body. And þe fyne rubie is founde in þe londe of libie in a flome þat comeþ owte of paradise; & he wole be seet in fyne gold. Also he makeþ a man welbelouid with lord & lady. Þe water þat it is wasshen yne, it distroyeþ þe moren of bestes & of men. Þe man þat bereþ þis ston schal be neuer ouercom in ple ne in batayl, & þis seyþ euax kyng & emperowr.

Ruby is a shining red stone, and he strengthens all stones that are red, as the book tells. The gentle ruby that is fine and pure is lord of all stones, and he is also like that water of waters. It has more virtue than all other precious stones, and he is of such lordship that when he who bears it comes among other men, they will all offer him honour and grace, and all men show joy at his coming. The book tells us that beasts who drink the water in which the ruby has been wetted will be whole of their sickness; and he who has discomfort in belief in God, and beholds this stone, it will comfort him and make him forget his contrariety by the virtue that God has given to it. It feeds a man and comforts his heart and his body, and it wins a man lordship. There are three great rubies, and they are found in the land of Libya in a river of paradise. Moses put this stone on the breast of Aaron in the second corner of the twelve stones. Also this stone cleanses the eyes and comforts the body. And the fine ruby is found in the land of Libya in the river that comes out of paradise; and he should be set in fine gold. Also he makes a man well beloved of his lord and lady. The water that it is washed in destroys murrain of beasts and men. The man who bears this stone will never be overcome in plea or in battle, and this says Evax king and emperor.

123. [Lychnite]

[fol. 15r] Letates is a ston, & it is lyk in color to an attercop or an yrene or a spider. He þat bereþ þis stone schal neuer be harmed with eny wenym, nor þe place þat he lyeþ yne. And yf a woman be ful of blod, bynd þis stone to her forhed with a lynen cloþe, & it schal staynche here. And yf a old man haue þis stone vpone him, þe mor he bloweþ þe feyre, þe mor schal it quenche.

Lychnite is a stone that is similar in colour to a spider or a piece of iron or a spider. He who bears this stone will never be harmed by any venom, nor the place that he lives in. And if a woman is full of blood, bind this stone to her forehead with a linen cloth, and it will staunch her. And if an old man has this stone upon him, the more he blows the fire, the more it will go out.

114. [Litharge]

Litugures is a stone þat þefendeþ mennes howses fro mysauentures boþe for man & woman; & yf a woman be in trauel of child, it schal helpe her if sche drinke it in powder.

Litharge is a stone that defends men's houses from misadventures both for men and women; and if a woman is in labour with a child, it will help her if she drinks it as a powder.

125. [Lynx]

Lincis is a stone of þe dace, þat if a man be sike in his bely, grynd þis stone & drinke it with wyȝt wyne & he schal be hole. And yf a man haue withyne him la cursum men clepeþ, schal helpe him.

Lynx is a stone of Dacia. If a man is sick in his belly, grind this stone and drink it with white wine and he will be whole. And if a man has within him what men call *la cursum*, it will help him.

126. [Litharge]

Litigerus is a stone like to lede & siluer, but he haþe litel vertu.

Litharge is a stone similar to lead and silver, bit he has has little virtue.

127. [Odontelicius][121]

Lontucerius is a stone, & he is profitable for a man þat wil tak venison priuely, & for huntyng & for fowling.

Odontelicius is a stone which is profitable for a man who wants to take venison secretly, and for hunting and for fowling.

128. [Lapis Lazuli]

Lasulus is a stone þat is a stone ryȝt gode for medecyns; & also yf a man haue þe feuer quartene, take & grynd þis stone & drynke it with water of rose, & he schal be hole þorowȝ þe vertu of þis stone.

Lapis lazuli is a stone very good for medicines; and also if a man has the quartan fever, take and grind this stone and drink it with rosewater, and he will be whole through the virtue of this stone.

129. [Malachite]

Molochites is a grene stone, & it is lyk to smaradus, but it is more boystous gren þen þe sma\ra/gdus, & so it haþe þe name after þe color of malues, as Ised seyd, & he is bred in araby. & he is ful nessh in substance, & neuer-þe-lesse it is ful profitable, as Diascorides seyþ, for it kepeþ & saueþ childryn fro noyfull yuelys & happes; & whoso bereþ it in his lyf syde, þer schal no wykkyd þynge greue him.

Malachite is a green stone, and it is similar to emerald, but it is a more lurid green than the emerald, and so it is named after the colour of mallows, as Isidore says, and he grows in Arabia. And he is very soft in substance, but nevertheless very profitable, as Dioscorides says, for it keeps and saves children from harmful evils and mishaps; and whoever bears it on his left side, no wicked thing will grieve him.

130. [Marble]

Marble is clepid marmor, & he haþe þe name of grekes for gren-esse, as Ised seyþ. Also marbole ben noble stons, & þey ben prysed for speckes of diuerse colors, for marble is endless; & þer bene

Marble is called *marmor*, and he has amongst the Greeks a reputation for greenness, as Isidore says. Also marbles are noble stones, and they are prized for spots of different colours, for

---

[121] Otherwise known as Wolf's Tooth.

þerof many maner of kendes, but þey ben not all hewen owte of rokk. And þer bene maner of marbles as it is founde in many dyuers landes & places vnder þe erþe, as marble of lacedomonia, & þat is grene & precius, & þat marble is cleped ophites, for it is specked like an edder. Marble purpurices comeþ owte of egypt, & it is rody with punctes amonge, & it haþe þat name purpurices, for he is red as purpil. And þer bene many maners of kynde of marble, as alabastrum & parium, & of him we shul speke ynner mor. Also a-noder maner of kynde is cleped coralicitum, & it is founde in asia, & it passeþ not ij cubites in mesure, & it is wyȝt as yuory, & some han wyȝt speckes in dyuerse proposions. Also anoþer kynde is cleped telaicum, & it is spreynt with golden speckes, & it is founde in de contrey of egipt, & it is kendly schapen to make þerone colliria & oynemenes þat helpen yene. Oder kendes of marble breden in qwarreis & in roches, as marble þat is clepid marble dounche, & þerof is made pilors & pawmentes & towres; also þer is anoþer maner kynde which is cleped charistium, & it is grene & beest; & it haþe þe name of aspeton, for men þat grauen loue it wel for þe gren color, for it comforteþ wel þe syȝt. Also þer is anoder kynde þat is cleped virundicum, & it groweþ in india, & it makeþ þyng þat is froted with lyke to gold, & þerfor it haþe þat

marble is endless; and there are many kinds, but they are not all hewed out of rock. And there are kinds of marble that are found in many different lands and places under the earth, such as marble of Sparta, which is green and precious; and that marble called *ophite*, because it is speckled like an adder. Purple marble comes out of Egypt, and it is reddish with spots among, and it has that name purple because he is red like purple. And there are many kinds of marble, such as alabaster and Parian, and of him we will speak more further in. Also another kind is called coralicite, and is found in Asia, and it is never larger than two cubits in size, and it is as white as ivory, and has some white specks in different pro-portions. Also, another kind is called *telaicum*, and it is sprinkled with gold spots, and it is found in the country of Egypt, and it is suitably shaped to make eye salves and ointments that help the eyes on it. Other kinds of marble grow in quarries and in rocky places, such as the marble which is called dounch marble, from which pillars, pavements and towers are made. Also there is another kind which is called *charistium*, and it is green and of the best; and it has the name *aspeton*, for men who engrave love it very much for the green colour, for it comforts the sight greatly. Also there is another kind which is called *virundicum*, and it name; also Ised seyþe, li° xvj; and þer he setteþ an ensample of many dyuerse marble, is mor sade, mor hard, mor stronge & feyre, mor profitable þen oþer stones. In þe veynes þerof þer is founden diuerse materes as ben precios stones; for þe hardnes þerof is most hard to grauen, & for cold & sondynes þerof it is best to kepe in spicire & oynementes ouer all oder þynges. We may wonder þat marble stones be not hewen ne clouen with yerne ne with stele ne with hamer ne with sawe, as þey ben with a plate of lede ysete betwyx nessh shynglis eiþer spones, for with led & with yere marble stones ben hewe & ycloven & Iplaned as for small stones.

grows in India, and it makes something that is rubbed on it like gold, and therefore it has that name. Also Isidore describes it in his sixteenth book; and there he sets down examples of many different kinds of marble, which is more rigid, harder, stronger, fairer and more profitable than other stones. In the veins of it are found different materials that are precious stones; for the hardness of it is most hard to engrave, and on account of the coldness and soundness of it it is better than all other things to keep spices and ointments in. We may marvel that marble stones are neither hewed nor split with iron or steel, hammer or saw, but with a plate of lead set between soft shingles on either side; for with lead and with [*meaning uncertain*] marble stones are hewed and split and planed for small stones.

131. [Toadstone]

[fol. 15v] Noset crapendien is a precios stone, somdell wyhi3t, and þerof ben diuerse colores; and it is seyd þat þis ston is taken owte of þe todes hede, & it is then clensed in stronge wyne & water, as Dias seyþe. And sometyme þe schape of þe tode semeþ þerin, with schappen fete & brod. Þis stone helpit a3ens by3tynges of serpentes & of crepyng wormes, & a3ens venym, for in presense of venym he varyeþ, & brenneþ his

Toadstone is a precious stone, somewhat white, and there are different colours of it; and it is said that this stone is taken out of the toad's head, and it is then cleaned in strong wine and water, as Dioscorides says. And sometimes the shape of the toad seems to be within it, with broad and shaped feet. This stone helps against the biting of serpents and crawling snakes, and against venom, for in the presence of figures[122] þat towcheþ hi*m*, & schold boþe be yclosed y fer as dias seyþe.

venom he changes, and burns those fingers which touch him; and he should be enclosed in iron, as Dioscorides says.

132. [Niger]

Nige*r* is a stone, & me*n* clepe*n* it galantice*n*. Þe ve*r*tu of þis stone is þat yf a ma*n* hold it i*n* his mowþe, or ley it one his to*n*ge, & put hi*m* i*n* wax or i*n* ho*n*y, what ma*n* þat will hi*m* harme schall haue no power but come to hi*m* & telle hi*m*. And he þat bereþ hi*m* schal be loved of all me*n*, & his ve*r*tues i*n*crese. And yf a ma*n* will assay him, bynde þis stone vpon*e* her reynes, & þer schall neu*er* woman leye aȝen*s* her wyll; and if a ma*n* may not do his kende, bynde it to his naked flessh, & he schall do so myche þat þe rede blod schal come after. Ȝit yf þu wylt p*r*eue þis ston*e* better, take þis stone & put mylk i*n* hony togeder, & anoy*n*t þee, & þer schall no fley towche þe aft*er*.

Niger is a stone that men called *galanticum*. The virtue of this stone is that if a man holds it in his mouth, or lays it on his tongue, and puts him in wax or honey, whichever man who wills him harm will have no power, but will come to him and tell him. And he who bears him will be loved by all men, and his virtues will increase. And if a man wants to test him, bind this stone on her kidneys, and a woman will never lie against her will; and if a man may not perform his nature, bind it to his naked flesh, and he will do so much that the red blood will come after. Yet if you want to prove this stone better, take this stone and put milk in honey together, and anoint yourself, and no fly will touch you afterwards.

133. [Glass]

Uytru*m* is glas in englyssh. Ysed seyþe þat þis glasse is a ston*e* somdel whiȝt, & he may be hewe & cloue, & he is ful cler*e*. It dissolueþ, te*m*pereþ, & draweþ, & clenseþ & wasteþ sup*er*fluitte of humo*r*s. Also Ised seyde, I° xvj° cc° ij°, þat uytru*m* haþe þat name

Vitrum is 'glass' in English. Isidore says that this glass is a stone somewhat white, and he may be hewed and split, and he is very transparent. It dissolves, tempers and draws, and purifies and destroys superfluity of humours. Also Isidore says in the

---

[122] Evans and Serjeantson read 'fi[*n*]gres'.

of þe contre of uytrea in egypt; & þerof medecyns ben made, & þerwith bodyes & clodes ben wasschen. Þe kynd þerof is not fer fro þe kende of salt, & it is mad ryȝt as salt in drynes in old clyues. Þe soome[123] þerof is cleped affronicum, & it is genderd of þe droppyng of dowues in þe contre of asie, after it is dryed with þe hete of þe sone; & when it is best dryed þen it is schynyng as Ised seyþe. And Platea seith that uitrum is a veyne of þe erþe & it is hote & drey, lyȝt rede oþer wyȝt or citrin, & it is better sower, & somdell salt in sauor. Uytrum abateþ fatnes if it is taken in þe mowþe, & consumeþ & wasteþ glyme humors. Þe powder þerof confecte in claretyd hony worshipeþ þe fase, & clenseþ scabbes & qwiter of þe stomak & of þe guttes, if it come of a postome; & it clenseþ luys & scabbes of þe hede, & it sleeþ wormes of þe eeren, & it chenseþ[124] most perfite þe qwyter & scabbes; & put vynegar þerto, & it helpeþ gnawengeþ & swellyng. Also it helpeþ aȝens þe dropsi, & clenseþ dymnes of yene, if it is medeld with hony; & it sleeþ hony venim & distroyeþ it, & withstondeþ myȝtly þe palsy of þe tong, as platearius seyþ. Also dias seyþ þat uytrum is hote & drye in þe ende of þe þryd degree. And it laxeþ & clenseþ, as Ised

second chapter of the sixteenth book, that *vitrum* has that name from the country of Vitrea in Egypt; and medicines are made from it, and bodies and clothes are washed with it. The nature of it is not far from the nature of salt, and it is made as right as salt in the dryness of old rock fissures. The whole of it is called *afronicum*, and it is formed from the dropping of dew in the country of Asia, after it is dried with the heat of the sun; and when it is dried best it shines, as Isidore says. And Platearius says that *vitrum* is a vein of the earth and it is hot and dry, light red or otherwise white or citrine, and it is bitter sour, and somewhat salty in flavour. *Vitrum* reduces obesity if it is taken in the mouth, and consumes and destroys glum humours. The powder of it mixed with clarified honey honours the face, and cleans scabs and discharge of the stomach and of the guts, if it comes out of an impostume; and it cleanses lice and scabs on the head, and it slays worms of the ears, and it cleanses most perfectly the discharge and scabs; and put vinegar on it, and it helps griping and swelling. Also it helps against the dropsy, and purifies dimness of the eyes if it is mixed with honey; and it slays venom and destroys it, and mightily withstands the palsy of the tongue, as Platearius says.

---

[123] Evans and Serjeantson read '[f]oome'
[124] Evans and Serjeantson read 'c[l]enseþ'.

seyþe. Also glas, as auycen seyþ, is amonge stones as a fowle amonge men, for it receyueþ al maner of colors & peyntynges. & it is cleped vitrum for vy, his vertu, is bry3t & cler & ly3t schinyng, & þorow3 all þat is conceyued in [*illeg.*] in metayl & in vaynes of erþe whiche is hidde. Al maner licor is seene owteward, as it is wyne, & is yschewed as it wer to yen closed þat loke þeroone, as Ised seyþe. Also glas was fyrst yfonde besydes tholamayda, in þe clyfe besydes þe reuer þat spryngeþ owte of þe fote of þe monteyn of carmelo, whiles þe chepmen reyned; þerfor vpone þe grauell vpone þat reyne shypmen mad feyre of clottes ymedeled with bry3t grauell, & þerof rane stremes of new leycor þat was þe begynnyng of glas, as Ised seyþe. Now glas is mad of asshen of trees & of erbes with full stronge blastes of feyre, with þe wiche it is nowe medeld with now glas, now bras, now boþe torned into glas. When glas is Imolten in þe fornes & perfy3tly clensed, þen he takeþ puernes, bry3tnes & clernes. Glas is died **[fol. 16r]** with al maner of colors, so þat it foloweþ iacinctus, smaragdus, & oþer precios stones in color & bry3tnes. Also it is pleyant, so þat it receyueþ ful sone dyuerse & contrarie schappis by blast of þe glasier; & it is sometyme ybete & somtyme ygraue as siluer. Also Ised seyþe þat no metal is mor able to make of mirrores þen is

Also Dioscorides says that *vitrum* is hot and dry in the extremity of the third degree. And it loosens and cleanses, as Isidore says. Also glass, as Avicenna says, is to stones as a bird is to men, for it receives all manner of colours and pigments, and it is called *vitrum* for vi, his virtue, is bright and clear and light shining, and through all that is conceived in [*illeg.*] in metal and in the veins of the earth in which it is hidden. All kinds of liquid have the outward appearance of wine, and are shown to closed eyes that look upon it, as Isidore says. Also glass was first found beside Ptolemaida, in the cliff beside the river that springs out of the foot of Mount Carmel, while the seamen reigned. Therefore on the gravel during that reign, seamen made fire from turf mingled with bright gravel, and from it ran streams of a new liquid that was the beginning of glass, as Isidore says. Now glass is made of wood ash and herbs with very strong blasts of fire, by which it is mixed now with glass, now brass, now both turned into glass. When glass is melted into forms and perfectly cleansed, then he receives purity, brightness and transparency. Glass is dyed with all kinds of colours, so that it follows jacinth, emerald and other precious stones in colour and brightness. Also it is pliant, so that it very soon receives different and contrary shapes by the blast of the glazier; and it is sometimes beaten glas, neyþer to receyue peynture; but it is most worthid wyȝh glas ȝat is nyx to cristall in color; For it is oft ychose befor siluer & gold to drinke in, as Ised seyþ. Also þis he seyþ, þat þe stone Osianus is rekened amonge þe kend of glas, & þis ston is somtyme grene & somtyme glas, & it is cler & bryȝt, & it is cleped Speclaris & is with fatti liȝt. Of þis stone many men maken precios stones, & to contrefet, as Ised seyþ. And al glas haþ þis propirte, þat it is most plyant whiles it is in meltyng hote & nessh, & it is most brotel when it is cold & hard, & yf it be brok it may not be amended withowt meltyng aȝen. But þer was oone had mad plyant glas þat myȝt be amended and wrowȝt with hamer. Also Ised seyþ þat oone browȝt a wiole made of such glas befor tiberius þe emperor, & þrew it down aȝen þe grownde, & was not ibroke but Ibend & yfold, & he riȝthed it & amended it with a hamer; þen þe emperor let smyt of his hed anone, lest, if þat craft wer Iknow, gold schold be worse þen glas, & oþer metal schold be litel worþe. For sikerly if glas were not brotel, it schold be aconted mor worþe þen a wessel of gold, as Ised seyþ. Þen glas is clene & pure, & specialy bryȝt & clere, & ymages & schadowes ben seyne þerin; & it is plyant when it is molten & hote, & brotel when it is cold & hard; & it receyueþ al color; & it foloweþ precios stones more in color þen in walew, & it

and sometimes engraved, like silver. Also Isidore says that no metal is able to make mirrors as glass can, nor to receive pigmentation; but the most worthy white glass is near to crystal in colour. For it is often chosen before gold and silver to drink in, as Isidore says. Also he says this: that the stone obsidian is reckoned a kind of glass, and this stone is sometimes green and sometimes glassy, and is clear and bright, and is called *specularis* and is with fatty light. Of this stone many men make precious stones, and counterfeit, as Isidore says. And all glass has the property that it is most pliant and soft while molten, and it is most brittle when it is cold and hard; and if it is broken it may not be mended without melting it again. But there was one who had made pliant glass that might be altered and wrought with a hammer. Also Isidore says that one man brought a vial made of such glass before Tiberius the emperor, and threw it down on the ground; and it was not broken but bent and folded; and he corrected and mended it with a hammer. Then the emperor allowed his head to be cut off shortly after, lest, if that craft were known, gold should be worse than glass, and other metals of little worth. For certainly, if glass were not brittle, it should be considered more valuable than a vessel of gold, as Isidore says. Glass is clean and pure, and especially bright and

clenseþ fylþe & superfluite.
Auycen seyþe þe powder þerof
clenseþ teþe & doþe away welkes
of yene; & it helpeþ gretly aȝens
þe stone of þe blader & of þe
reynes, yf it be dronk with wyne.

clear, and images and shadows are
seen in it, and it is pliant when it
is molten and hot, and brittle
when it is cold and hard; and it
receives all colours, and it follows
precious stones more in colour
than in value, and it cleanses filth
and superfluity. Avicenna says
that powder of it cleans teeth and
does away lesions of the eyes; and
it helps greatly against the stone
of the bladder and of the kidney if
it is drunk with wine.

134. [Orite]

Orides is a stone of color, & he is
gode aȝens venym & aȝens
byȝtyng of wode bestes; and he
þat bereþ it vpone him may
sikerly goo þorow desertes &
hermytagies. Anoþer maner is
had, & þat is grene & it haþe wyȝt
ioyntes, & heleþ a man fro
contrariosnes; also in goote of þe
syde he is scharp vpone þat oþer
syd; he is pleyne. Þe woman þat
bereþ him may conceyue no child,
& if sche be with chyld sche schal
lese her chyld.

Orite is a coloured stone who is
good against venom and against
biting of woodland beasts; and he
who bears it upon him may go
with safety through deserts and
lonely places. There is another
kind that is green and has white
branches, and heals a man from
contrariness; also in [meaning
uncertain] of the side he is sharp
on the other side; he is plain. The
woman who bears him may
conceive no child, and if she is
with child she will lose her child.

135. [Onyx]

Onicle is a stone þat comeþ owte
of ynd & of Arabie; & Onycle,
Sardius & calcidine ben drawing
togeder. Onycle kepeþ a man
hardy, coragies & wroþe. And yf
he bere him in his fynger or abowt
his nyke, he kepeþ him saaf &
encreseþ his bewte. Þe onycle is
blak of color & his vertu is in

Onyx is a stone that comes out of
India and Arabia; and onyx,
sardine and chalcedony draw
together. Onyx keeps a man bold,
courageous and angry. And if he
bears him on his finger or around
his neck, he keeps him safe and
increases his beauty. Onyx is
black in colour, and his virtue is in

gold. He doeþ away fantaȝies, & makeþ a man to hawe gret dremes, & he makeþ a man hardy in fyȝt; & he helpeþ a man in plee, & so to conquer his ryȝt; & he wole not be myche loke þerone. Midas þe boke telleþ vs it makeþ a man to speke to his dede frend by nyȝt in metyng; & if it fal to drem in þe morow, þen þe dede is in travel. He þat bereþ it schal haue many gode graces. Þe bible seyþe þat þe Onycle was in þe fowerþ corner of þe brest of arone.

gold. He does away fantasies, and makes a man have great dreams, and he makes a man bold in combat, and he helps a man in plea, and this to obtain his right; and he will not be much looked upon. The book Midas tells us that it allows a man to speak to his dead friend by night in a meeting; and if it has failed to bring a dream by the next day, then the one dead is in torment. He who bears it will have many good graces. The Bible says that onyx was in the fourth corner of the breast of Aaron.

136. [Opal]

Optalio is a stone þat is cleped opalus. Also it is a stone distingned with colores of diuerse precios stones, as Ised seyþe, þat þerin is þe feyr of carbuncle, þe schynyng purpur of þe amatist, þe bryȝt color of þe smaragdus, & colors schynen þeryne with a maner dyuersite of þe contrey of ynde in wyhche he is brede; and it is trowed þe[125] he haþe as many vertues as colors. Of þis optallio it is seyde in þe lapidary þat he kepeþ & saueþ yene, & kepeþ him cler & scharp & withowte greuance; and þer is a syknes þat blyndeþ menis yen with a maner of clowde & smyteþ him with a

Optalio is a stone that is called opal. Also it is a stone distinguished by the colours of different precious stones, as Isidore says; therein is the fire of carbuncle, the shining purple of amethyst, the bright colour of emerald, and the colours shine in it with a kind of diversity from the country of India in which he grows. And it is stated that he has as many virtues as colours. Of this opal it is said in the lapidary that he keeps and preserves eyes, and keeps them clear and sharp and without disease; and there is a sickness that blinds men's eyes with a kind of cloud and strikes him down with a kind of blindness

---

[125] Read 'þat'?

maner blyndnes which is cleped anancia, so þat þey mow not se neyþer to take hede wat is befor her yene; **[fol. 16v]** þerfor it is seyd þat he most sikere pattron of þeves, as seyþe þe lapidary.

which is called *anancia*,[126] so that they cannot see, nor take heed of what is before their eyes; therefore it is said that he is the most certain patron of thieves, as the lapidary says.

137. [Orite]

Orites is a stone, & þer-of ben iij maners; þat one is blak, þat oþer is lyke hony or waxe, þe iij is gren with blak spekkes. He þat bereþ þis ston shall neuer have harme of beest. Yf þu will preue þis ston, þrow him into þe feyre; yf þu may fynd him, kepe him wel, for þat is þe ryȝt orist.[127] Þe þryd ston kepit knowlech; he is like hony in þat one syde, þat oþer part is pleyne & lyȝt, & in þe oþer part playne as it were a clouce.[128] He þat bereþ schal neuer gete chyld, ne no woman conceyue while it is vpone him; & yf a woman be trauelyng of chyld, sche schal soone be delyuerd weþer sche will or will not.

Orite is a stone of which there are three kinds: one is black, the other is like honey or wax; the third is green with black specks. He who bears this stone will never be harmed by a beast. If you want to prove this stone, throw him into the fire; if you can find him, keep him well, for that is the right origin. The third stone preserves knowledge; he is like honey on one side; the other side is plain and light, and plain on the other side like a boulder. He who bears it will never beget a child, nor will any woman conceive while it is upon her; and if a woman is labouring with child, she will soon be delivered whether she wants it or not.

138. [Pyrite]

Pirite is a stone, þat whoso draweþ him he will not abyd with him. His kend is to be towched lyȝtly, & he most hold it softly in his honde; & yf a man streyn him hard he wol bren his hond; or fret

Pyrite is a stone that whoever draws him will not be able to abide. His nature is to be touched lightly, and he must hold it softly in his hand; and if a man strains him hard he will burn his hand; or

---

[126] Probably an allusion to cataracts, from the name of the biblical character Ananias, who heals St Paul of temporary blindness in the Book of Acts.

[127] Read 'oriȝt'?

[128] Read 'cloude'?

him one his fynger, his fynger schall bren. Pirite is red ly3t, lyk to þe qualyte of þe eyre; myche feyre is þer-in, & oft sprynges to men owte þerof. And he haþe his name of pire, þat is to sey feyre.

if he rubs him on his finger his finger will burn. Pyrite is light red, similar to the quality of the air; much fire is within it, and it often springs out of it at men. And he has this name of *pyros*, that is to say, fire.

139. [Paeanite]

Piante is a stone þat comeþ owte of macedony of þe kyngdom; & he is god for womans kende, for he makeþ lytel labore of woman, & he is gode for a woman ~~kend~~ þat conceyueþ, & makeþ a woman to chyld, & he is myche helpyng to þe fadere & to þe moder, & it is god for wraþe.

Paeanite is a stone that comes out of the kingdom of Macedonia; and he is good for womankind, for he makes small labour for women, and he is good for women for conceive, and makes a woman with child, and he is much help to the father and mother; and it is good for wrath.

140. [Prase]

Prassio is a stone, & it comeþ owte of macedony of þat kyngdome; and he is god for womans kend, for he makeþ lytel þe labur of women, for he ~~he~~ is good for conceyuyng, & it makeþ a woman sone to have chyld. Also he helpeþ mych to þe fader & moder; and it is good a3ens wraþ. Þis ston prassio is grene as leke, & he comforteþ myche þe sy3t; & he is founde sometyme with red droppes, & sometyme dystyngned with wy3t dropes. Of þis stone it is seyd in bokes þat no profite is þerwith but þat he is grene, & wyrschypeþ mych gold.

Prase is a stone that comes out of the kingdom of Macedonia; and he is good for womankind, for he makes small the labour of women, for he is good for conceiving, and makes a woman have a child soon. Also he helps greatly the father and mother; and it is good against wrath. This stone prase is green like a leek, and he greatly comforts the sight; and he is sometimes found with red spots, and sometimes distinguished with white spots. It is said of this stone in books that there is no profit in it except that he is green, and greatly honours gold.

141. [Panteros]

Panteros is a stone, & comeþ of a best þat haþe many colors. If a man bere þis stone, it is god for yuel neyȝbores. Þis ston panterone is of dyuers colors ysprenge & dystyngned dyuersly; also he is seyne blak, rede, gren, pale purpil & ȝelowȝ, & also bryȝt gren in colour. And þis stone makeþ a man bold & hardy, so þat he schal not be ouercome þat day þat he seeþ him ȝerly at þe sone reysyng, as it is seyd in dyuers bokes.

Panteros is a stone that comes from a beast that has many colours. If a man bears this stone, it is good for evil neighbours. This stone panteros is of different colours scattered and variously distinguished; also he is seen in black, red, green, pale purple and yellow, and also as bright green in colour. And this stone makes a man bold and hardy, so that he will not be overcome on that day when he sees him annually at sunrise, as it is said in many books.

142. [Drosolite]

Prosultes is a stone þat haþ þe same vertu þat þe flent haþe, for he wole tende feyre.

Drosolite is a stone that has the same virtue as flint has, for he will ignite fire.

143. [Parian Marble]

Parius is a stone of þe kend of þe noble & gentil marbul, for he [is] precios. Also Ised seyþ þat ston is founde in þe lond of paroun, & þerfor it is cleped paryus. Þe quantite þerof passeþ lances & [*illeg.*] & it is good to kepe in spycery & oynementes. Also Ised seyþ, & þe glose vpon ester seyþ, þat parius is a kend of most whiȝt marbul, & þerfor it be token of chasitte.[129]

Parian is a stone of the kind of noble and gentle marble, for he is precious. Also Isidore says that this stone is found in the land of Paros, and therefore it is called Parian. The quantity of it surpasses lances and [*illeg.*] and it is good to keep spices and ointments in. Also Isidore says, and the Gloss on Esther says, that Parian is a kind of most white marble, and therefore it betokens chastity.

---

[129] Evans and Serjeantson read 'chas[ti]te'.

144. [Paeanite]

Proinces is a stone of femal kend, as it is seyd, for somtyme he conceyueþ & bereþ such anoþer stone. Also he helpeþ women þat ben with child, as Dias seyþ.

Paeanite is a stone of female gender, so it is said, for sometimes he conceives and bears another such stone. Also he helps women who are with child, as Dioscorides says.

145. [Peridot]

Periot is a stone þat is ly3t grene.

Peridot is a stone that is light green.

BIBLIOGRAPHY

Manuscript

Cambridge University Library MS Peterborough Cathedral 33, fols 1r–16v

Edition of the Peterborough Lapidary

Evans, J. and Serjeantson, M. S. (eds), *Mediaeval English Lapidaries*, Early English Texts Society 190 (Oxford: Early English Texts Society, 1933), pp. 10–11, 62–118, 160–79

Other sources

Bloomfield, J., 'Aristotelian Luminescence, Thomistic Charity: Vision, Reflection and Self-love in "Pearl"', *Studies in Philology* 108:2 (2011), pp. 165–88

Chumbley, A. D., *The Leaper Between: An Historical Study of the Toad-bone Amulet* (Three Hands Press, 2012)

Copenhaver, B. P., *Magic in Western Culture: From Antiquity to the Enlightenment* (Cambridge: Cambridge University Press, 2015)

Davenport, T., 'Jewels and Jewellers in "Pearl"', *The Review of English Studies*, New Series 59:241 (2008), pp. 508–20

Dean, R. J., *Anglo-Norman Literature: A Guide to Texts and Manuscripts* (London: Anglo-Norman Texts Society, 1999)

Doob, P., 'Chaucer's "Corones Tweyne" and the Lapidaries', *The Chaucer Review* 7:2 (1972), pp. 85–96

Dourish, E. and Hale, W., 'Incunabula on the Increase: the development of Cambridge University Library's incunabula collections after 1954', *Transactions of the Cambridge Bibliographical Society* 15:1 (2012), pp. 165–74

Duffin, C. J., 'Fish Otoliths and Folklore: A Survey', *Folklore* 118:1 (2007a), pp. 78–90

Duffin, C. J., 'The Cock's Stone', *Folklore* 118:3 (2007b), pp. 325–41

Forbes, R. J., *Studies in Ancient Technology* (Leiden: Brill, 1955–64), 9 vols

Foreman, P., *The Cambridge Book of Magic: A Tudor Necromancer's Manual* (Cambridge: Texts in Early Modern Magic, 2015)

Fredell, J. 'Alchemical Lydgate', *Studies in Philology* 107:4 (2010), pp. 429–64

Friis-Jensen, K. and Willoughby, J. M. W. (eds), *Peterborough Abbey*, Corpus of British Medieval Library Catalogues 8 (London: British Academy, 2001)

Fulk, R. D. and Cain, C. M. (eds), *A History of Old English Literature* (Oxford: Blackwell, 2003)

Harms, D., Clark, J. R. and Peterson, J. H. (eds), *The Book of Oberon: A Sourcebook of Elizabethan Magic* (Woodbury, MN: Llewellyn, 2015)

Henkin, L. J., 'The Carbuncle in the Adder's Head', *Modern Language Notes* 58:1 (1943), pp. 34–9

Keiser, G. R. (ed.), *The Middle English 'Boke of Stones': The Southern Version* (Brussels: Omirel, UFSAL, 1984)

Keiser, G. R., 'The Sources of the Peterborough Lapidary' in C. De Backer (ed.), *Cultuurhistorische Caleidoscoop: aangeboden aan Prof. Dr. Willy L. Braekman* (Ghent: Stichting Mens en Kultuur, 1992), pp. 342–8

Kelly, H. A., 'Canon Law and Chaucer on Licit and Illicit Magic', in Karras, R. M., Kaye, J. and Matter, E. A. (eds), *Law and the Illicit in Medieval Europe* (Philadelphia, PA: University of Pennsylvania Press, 2008), pp. 210–21

Manley, F., 'Chaucer's Rosary and Donne's Bracelet: Ambiguous Coral', *Modern Language Notes* 74:5 (1959), pp. 385–88

Page, S., *Magic in the Cloister: Pious Motives, Illicit Interests, and Occult Approaches to the Medieval Universe* (University Park, PA: Pennsylvania State University Press, 2013)

Riddle, J. M., 'Lithotherapy in the Middle Ages: Lapidaries considered as Medical Texts', *Pharmacy in History* 12:2 (1970), pp. 39–50

Taylor, P. B., 'Chaucer's Eye of the Lynx and the Limits of Vision', *The Chaucer Review* 28:1 (1993), pp. 67–77

Vising, J., *Anglo-Norman Language and Literature* (Oxford: Oxford University Press, 1923)

Walton, S. A., 'Theophrastus on *Lyngurium*: Medieval and Early Modern Lore from the Classical Lapidary Tradition', *Annals of Science* 58 (2001), pp. 357–79

Young, F., *A History of Exorcism in Catholic Christianity* (London: Palgrave MacMillan, 2016)

Young, F., '*Instruments of nigromancie*: materials of ritual magic in late medieval and early modern England' in Bosselmann-Ruickbie A. and Ruickbie L. (eds), *The Material Culture of Magic* (Leiden: Brill, forthcoming)

INDEX

This index refers in all cases to the translation rather than the original text. References given in bold are to illustrations.

Bartholomaeus Anglicus, lapidarist xvi, xix, 1, 3, 34
beams (of light) xxxiii, 10, 12, 14, 19, 21, 33, 44, 69, 74
bees 59
belioculus 18
bericia 17
beryl 15–17, 18, 36, 37
bezoar xxx
Bible
	see Scripture
bitumen 18
bladder xxxii, 89
blindness xxxii, 41, 77, 90–1
blisters xxxii, 26
bloodstone xviii, xxxvii, 5n., 40–1
bloody flux
	see haemorrhage;
	menstruation
Boke of Stones xviii–xx, xxi
boiling water
	stones that prevent 10, 75
	test for stones xxviii, 44, 75
boils xxxii, 65
Boyle, Robert, chemist xxx
brass 63, 69, 87
breastfeeding xxxii, 9, 22, 29, 23, 49–50
breastmilk 46, 77
Britain 47, 61, 76
burns 11, 17, 37, 45, 47, 62, 63, 85, 91–2

caladony 52
calastida 29
calciphane 28–9
calluca 22
calonite xxxix, 29–30

Cambridge University Library vii, xii, xix, xxi, xxiv
cameo 22
Cantimpré, Thomas of xvi
capnite xxxvii, 27
capon xviii, 8
carbuncle xxix, 32–4, 38, 66, 90
Carmel, Mount 87
carnelian 29
cataracts 77, 89, 90–1
cataricus 31
celidony xxvi, xl, 24, 32, 54–5
chalazias 50–1
chalcedony xxxix, xl, 20–1, 89
Chambers, John, Abbot and Bishop of Peterborough xxiii
charms xxxvii, 40, 41, 47
	see also enchantments;
	magic; witchcraft
chastity 23, 60, 68, 69, 72, 73, 93
Chaucer, Geoffrey, poet xvii
childbearing
	see pregnancy
childbirth
	see pregnancy
chilindris 22
chrysolite xviii, 19–20
chrysopase 34
chrysoprase 21
Cilicia 64
cimbria 26
cinaedia xviii, xxvi, 22, 26
Circe xxviii, xxxvii, 62
citrine 53, 56, 86
Civil War, English xxiii–xxiv
cock xvii, 8
colic xxxii, 12, 23
collorus xl, 27
conception xviii, xxix, xxxii, xxxiii, 8–9, 35, 43, 76, 87, 92

litharge 31, 49, 81
litharge of silver 15
lithomancy
    see divination; magic
lithotherapy
    see medicine
liver xxxii, 16, 17
Locke, John, philosopher xxx
London Lapidary of King
Phillip xvi, xviii
love xvii, xxxv, 5, 16, 17, 21,
24, 25, 30, 32, 39, 42, 62, 63,
70, 85
    see also marriage
lunacy 24, 75
lychnite 81
Lycia 47
Lydgate, John, poet xvii
Lyndwood, William, canonist
xxxvi
lyngurium 59–61
lynx (animal) 61
lynx (stone) 81

Macedonia 92
macedony 51
magic vii, xii, xiii–xv, xxviii,
xxx, xxxiii–xl
    astral xiv, xxxviii, xxx,
    xxxv, xxxvi, xxxviii
    counter-magic
        see witchcraft
    natural xii, xxxv, xxxvi
    ritual
        see
    necromancy
    sympathetic xxxv,
    xxxviii
    see also necromancy;
    witchcraft
magnet xxviii, xxxiii, xxxvii, 7,
62–4

malachite 82
mallows 82
Mandeville, Jean, lapidarist xvi
manuscript of the Peterborough
Lapidary
    language xxi
    provenance xxi–xxiv
    physical features xx
    scholarship on xv–xx
marble 82–4
    see also Parian marble
Marbod of Rennes, lapidarist
xiii, xv, xx, xxxv, xxxvii
marriage 17
Medes 77
medicine vii, xii, xiii, xiv, xv,
xxi, xxiv, xxv, xxx–xxxiii,
xxxvi
medus 77–8
melancholy 56, 66, 78
melichros 79
menstruation xxxii, 29, 48, 52,
60, 76
    see also bloody flux
Methodorus 24
Midas 90
Middle English vii, xvii, xviii,
xxi, xxvi, xlii–xliii
milk xxxiii, 48, 49, 65, 77, 85
    see also breastfeeding;
    breastmilk
mineralogy xiv, xv, xxix
miracles xxxv
mirrors xxxix, 38, 68, 69, 75,
78, 87–8
miscarriage 27, 47, 89
molas 59
monks, Benedictine xvii, xxi,
xxiii, xxiv, xxxv
moon xxxix, 13, 15, 21, 30, 59,
61, 73, 74, 75
    see also magic, astral

moonstone 14–15
Moses xxxvii, xxxviii, 4, 11, 16, 52, 60, 80
murrain xxxii, 80
myrrh 2, 3, 60, 121
myrrhite 121

nard 79
necromancy xxxiii, xxxv, xxxvii–xxxviii, xxxix, xl, 13, 28, 37, 53, 67, 90,
Nero, emperor xxxix, 38
niger xxxiii, 85
Nile, river 14
nitrate of lime 49–50
Norman French xiii
North Midland Lapidary xviii
Northamptonshire xxi, xxiv
Northgate, Michael, monk xxxv
nosebleeds xxxii, 66
nursing
        see breastfeeding

obesity xxxii, 86
obsidian 78–9, 88
oblyx 79
Ocean (Atlantic) 5, 51
odontelicius 82
ointment 31, 83, 84, 93
onyx xxvi, xxxvii, xxviii, xxxix, 20, 70, 71, 72, 78, 89–90
opal 90–1
orite 89, 91
otoliths xviii, 22, 26, 28, 38, 41, 53, 84

paeanite xxix, 92, 94
palsy xxxii, 38, 45, 65, 86
panteros 93
Parian marble 93

Paros 93
pearl xvii, 25, 68, 75–6
Pearl (Middle English poem) xv, xvii
peridot 94
Persia 30, 72
Peterborough
        Abbey of xxi, xxiii
        Cathedral **vi**, vii, **xxv**
                library xii, xx xxiv
                sacked xxiii–xxiv
poison xxx, xxxviii, 27, 42, 52, 57, 61
        see also venom
phantoms 53
pharmacology
        see apothecaries; medicine
Philadelphus 74
Philosophers' Stone xvii
Phytonas 25
piercing of stones 19, 21, 26, 27, 29, 36, 49, 54, 76
Platearius xvi, 63, 86
Plato 76
Pliny the Elder xii, xvi, xxvi, 1, 2n., 74
poaching 82
prase 34, 92
prasina
pregnancy xxxii, xxxiii, 5, 9, 27, 29, 32, 35, 42, 43, 45, 47, 48, 49, 51, 52, 81, 89, 91, 92, 94
        see also conception; miscarriage
Ptolemaida 87
purgatory 90
pyrite xxxvii, 15, 37, 91–2

Quendis, river 59
quinsy xxxii, 55
quirine 57

raven 58
recipe literature xiii, xxi, xxxiii
Red Sea 5, 13, 24, 43, 58
Renaissance xxxvi
rheum xxxii, 29
Richard Rufus, lapidarist 1
riches xxxix, 5, 14, 20, 35, 38,
42, 69, 70
rings xiv, 17, 25, 54, 58, 63,
64, 71, 78, 89
ritual magic
    see magic; necromancy
roses, oil of 27, 31
rosewater 82
ruby xxxviii, 10n., 80–1
    see also balas ruby;
        spinel ruby

sacraments xxxix, xl, 24
saliva 78
salt 29, 50, 69, 86
sapphire xxvi, xxviii, xxix,
xxxiv, xxxv, xxxvii, xxxix, 13,
19, 27, 34, 56, 57, 64–8
sardine xxxvii, xxxix, 9, 10, 20,
70–1, 78, 89
sardis 70
sardonyx 72, 78
savin juniper 17, 45
scabies xxxiii, 31, 49, 50
scabs 86
science, medieval vii, xii, xiv,
xxxv–xxx
scorpion 7
Scripture 2, 16, 20, 39, 52, 60,
65, 70, 71, 73, 74, 90
scrying xxxix
    see also divination

Scythia 53, 68
seafaring 74, 87
seawater 19, 20, 27
serpent's tongue
    see toadstone
serpentine xxvi, xxxviii, 61,
72–3
sex 9
    see also conception;
        contraception;
        impotence; lechery;
        love
sheep 11, 29, 46, 49, 50, 77
shellfish 75
Sicily 2
silver xxxviii, 5, 13, 15, 37, 53,
61, 77, 81, 88
sin xxxix, 1, 7, 19, 20, 22
singing 11
sleep 7, 26, 31, 57, 79
snakes 3, 7, 28, 48, 84
    adder 27, 47, 53, 83
    asp 53
    see also worms
sores 9, 31
Spain 51
Sparta 83
spider xxviii, 67, 81
spinel 10
spinel ruby 43
spleen 17, 63, 64
spirits xviii, xxxvi, xxxvii,
xxxviii–xxxix, xl, 7, 11, 20, 21,
25, 27, 36, 37, 67, 69
static electricity
    see electrostatic
        properties
staunching xix, 25, 29, 40, 41,
48, 52, 54, 60, 66, 70, 75, 81
stomach complaints xxxiii, 17,
44, 48, 60, 77, 81, 86

www.ingramcontent.com/pod-product-compliance
Lightning Source LLC
Chambersburg PA
CBHW031300310326
41914CB00116B/1720/J